FEARLESS LATIN:

A Gardener's Introduction to Botanical Nomenclature

Sara G. Mauritz

Contents

Preface

Fearless Latin did not start out to be a book. It originated as a series of articles published in *The Gardeners*, the member publication of Portland Garden Club (Oregon), over a period of ten or so years. My aim was to help fellow gardeners lose their reluctance to use botanical names for plants and leave behind the oft-poetic but far from precise common names . My basic tenet was that if you offered the readers small portions of botanical Latin and could demystify both the pronunciation and the meaning, that they would not be afraid to try.

Fearless Latin it not a comprehensive dictionary of botanical Latin terms, nor is it an encyclopedic reference work on the formal taxonomy of plants. It is instead an invitation to home gardeners, everywhere, to jump in to the world of binomial nomenclature, the proper name for botanical Latin, and learn what a wonderful tool it is. This tool allows people all over the world to talk about plants—where they come from, how they grow, what they look like, etc.—using the same language. There is nothing scary, nothing snobbish and certainly nothing silly about using botanical Latin to learn about plants.

I don't have a degree in botany or horticulture, I just love plants and I became fascinated with the amount of information that is available to the gardener when you use botanical Latin

Acknowledgments

My thanks first to my parents, Jean and Robert Grogan who imbued in me a love of plants, gardening and botanical Latin at a very young age. My thanks also to the members of The Portland Garden Club, who gave me both the forum in which to write "Fearless Latin" and the encouragement to keep going month after month and year after year. My deepest thanks to my daughter, Gwyn Mauritz, who was invaluable as a critic, editor, and artistic "eye" throughout the writing process for the original "Fearless Latin" columns. And, finally, my sincere thanks to my sister, Sandy Grogan Dresser, for facilitating the process of taking years of "Fearless Latin" to book form. Without her help, there would be no book.

Sara G. Mauritz
Portland, OR
Spring, 2011

Introduction

My introduction to botanical Latin started when I was a very small child following my father around the garden. He was a scientist by profession so it never occurred to him not to use the botanical names for the plants in the garden even to a three or four year old girl. From that early beginning gardening and botanical Latin have been a constant in my life. Another constant has been my frustration with common names for plants that vary so much from place to place. Have you ever noticed how many different plants are called Sunflowers? How about Strawberry begonia which is neither a strawberry nor a begonia but actually a Saxifage—botanically named *Saxifraga stolonifera.* Many common names were given to plants by people who knew nothing about plants but "thought" they looked sort of like something they knew in the "old country." Others were drawn from folklore and whimsy.

My primary goal in writing the *Gardeners' columns* was to enable the fearful, Latin-averse gardener to learn some basic terms, to become comfortable pronouncing them out loud and to use them. The original *Fearless Latin* columns have been edited and in some cases rearranged to make more sense in book form starting with some basics and moving along to more general information about plants but keeping the emphasis on the names and their meanings.

Throughout the book I use the term botanical Latin and it is important to understand what I mean by that is the proper name for plants. The system of naming plants scientifically was begun by Carl Linnaeus, an 18th Century Swedish naturalist. He devised a system for naming not only plants but animals and minerals as well. His system is known as binomial nomenclature and simply means that things are classified using two names —the Genus and the Species.

A genus of plants with similar characteristics may have one only species or literally thousands of species in it. But all members of a genus share a great many similarities. Within a genus we find plants which share the traits of the genus but also exhibit differences. We will discuss all this in depth in the ensuing chapters, but the very beginning lies in the two names: the genus (always capitalized) and the species (never capitalized). Using the example above: *Saxifraga stolonifera*, *Saxifraga* is the genus and *stolonifera* is the specific epithet or species name.

Botanists using DNA testing techniques have been busy reclassifying plants. Today some of the plants in the book may have been renamed. No effort has been made to keep up with the scientists in the field.

I hope my little book succeeds in spurring your interest in knowing the "real" names of plants and learning all that the botanical names can tell you.

The Basics

Making Sense of Latin

I'm often asked, "How can you remember all those Latin names?" I wish I had a dollar for every time I'm asked that question. By now I'd have a nice lovely slush fund to spend on plants. The answer comes in two parts. First, you have to want to use them. Then, you must make them meaningful to you. Sometimes I think the first decision—to use the scientific botanical name rather than the common one is the hardest to make. However, once made, you'll then find ways to make the Latin meaningful to you and therefore easier to remember.

Let's assume you're ready to learn and use the scientific names. First, take the plants that are old friends of yours and learn their scientific names. Then, when you're shopping for plants or visiting gardens, ask for the scientific names. Ignore the common names. As your botanical vocabulary grows you'll begin to see the patterns in nomenclature.

Sometime, just for fun, read the index of books such as the Random House series on Shrubs, Perennials, Bulbs, etc. Notice how many specific names end with root words like *-folius -a, -um* or *-phyllus -a, -um*, (the Latin and Greek words for leaf) and how many plants are identified by the characteristics of their leaves.

Generally these names fall into a few categories such as:
- the numbers of leaves,
- the width of the leaves,
- the size of the leaves,
- the shape of the leaves,
- if they look like some other plant's leaves, and the like.

Recognizing that the name describes the leaves is half the battle. Now you just need to add some descriptive terms to your vocabulary. For instance: leaf widths are often ***angustifolius*** (an-gus-ti-FOL-ee-us) [thin] and ***latifolius*** (la-ti-FOL-ee-us) [broad] or ***stenophyllus*** (ste-noh-FIL-us) [thin] and ***platyphyllus*** (pla-ti-FIL-us) [fat].

Big or small could be *longifolius* (lon-ji-FOL-ee-us) and *minutifolius* (mye-new-ti-FOL-ee-us) or *macrophyllus* (ma-kroh-FIL-us) and *microphyllus* (mye-kroh-FIL-us).

The majority of specific names describe plant parts. The other choices are names describing the geographic area where the plant was discovered or names commemorating the discoverer or someone he/she wanted to honor. You simply have to memorize those that fall into the latter group. But you can make the descriptive names meaningful to you by learning the Latin roots for basic plant parts, and then learning some basic descriptive terms.

I can almost hear your groans. But, this is exactly what we'll do in the following chapters. Just take your time; work on one plant part or one genus at a time, whichever works for you. Start with something you know from your own garden. If you can actually "see" the difference between a "something-or-other" *latifolia* and the same "something-or-other" *minutifolia* you'll be well on your way to making sense of scientific names.

Let me show you what I mean. The *Random House Book of Perennials* lists 16 different species of *Cardamine* (kar-DA-mi-nee)-all presumably civilized cousins of that little, white-flowered thug that sprays seeds around our gardens. Ten of those specific names describe the leaves:

diphylla (dye-FIL-a) -2 leaves

enneaphyllos (en-nee-a-FIL-us) -9 leaves

heptaphylla (hep-ta-FIL-us) -7 leaves

latifolia (la-ti-FOL-ee-us) -broad leaves

macrophylla (ma-kroh-FIL-a) -big leaves

microphylla (mye-kroh-FIL-a) -small leaves

pentaphyllus (pen-ta-FIL-us)-5 leaves from the Greek

quinquefolia (kwin-ke-FOL-ee-us) -5 leaves from the Latin

raphanifolia (ra-fan-i-FOL-ee-a) -leaves like a radish

trifolia (try-FOL-ee-a) -3 leaves

See how easy it can be? Here's another fun example of a doubly descriptive name, which incidentally combines both Greek and Latin elements: *Disanthus cercidifolius* (dis-AN-thus ser-si-di-FOL-ee-us). The name literally means a plant having no flowers or very insignificant ones with leaves that look like a *cercis* or redbud tree.

4

To learn your botanical Latin, it helps to have a gardener's dictionary on hand. Then you can learn the meaning of the name of your new plant as you put it into the ground. There are several good dictionaries on the market. *Gardener's Latin*, written by Bill Neal and published by Algonquin Books of Chapel Hill, NC is a nice little book to get you started. Then, when you really get serious, I recommend *Stearn's Dictionary of Plant Names for Gardeners*, by William T. Stearn and published by Cassell Publishers in London.

Challenge yourself. Make a game of botanical Latin. Break the names into parts you can remember. And, above all, don't fret about pronunciation. We'll look at pronunciation in the next chapter, but as long as you can spell it and know what it means, you'll be able to talk plants with any of the experts.

Pronouncing Botanical Latin

I've often thought that the biggest stumbling block in the use of botanical Latin is the uncertainty people have about how to pronounce these long complicated names. Well, take courage as we try to sort out the basic rules of pronunciation. As William T. Stearn's book, *Botanical Latin*, is accepted internationally as the standard reference work on the subject, I've chosen it for our source of information.

Part of the confusion about pronunciation stems from the fact that there are two main systems being used: the reformed academic (represented by Allen J. Coombes in his *Dictionary of Plant Names*) and the traditional English (generally used by gardeners and botanists including Michael Dirr in his *Manual of Woody Landscape Plants)*. The clearest differences are the hard *c* and the long *i* (which sounds like *ee* by the reformed academics group) and the greater use of long vowels (particularly in the endings) by the traditional English adherents.

Regardless of whether you prefer "stel-LAY-ta" or "stel-LAH-ta," you need to know where to put the accent or stress. Stearn outlines the rules for placement of the accent as follows:

- In Latin every vowel is pronounced, hence *co-to-ne-AS-ter* and not *cot-on-easter.* (This is true of the Latinized Greek words as well.)
- The stress or accent is on the first syllable in words with two syllables. Thus, *AL-bus, PLE-nus, MAG-nus.*
- The stress is on the <u>next to last</u> syllable in words with several syllables when:
    - the next to last syllable is long, as in *for-MO-sus,* or
    - two consonants separate the last two vowels, as in *cru-EN-tus.*
- The stress falls on the <u>second to last</u> syllable when the next to last syllable is short as in *FLO-ri-dus, la-ti-FOL-li-us,* or *sil-VAT-ti-cus.*
- Diphthongs (two vowels pronounced as one - *ae, au, ei, eu, oe, ui*) are considered long vowels. However, when two vowels come together without forming a diphthong in a Latin word, the first is short as in *CAR-ne-us,* but may be

long in a word of Greek origin like *gi-gan-TI-us*. The *inus* ending also varies sometimes being long and sometimes being short in both Latin and Greek.

These rules are sometimes difficult to apply to those generic and specific names that are not of Latin or Greek origin. Although there is a group of horticulturists today who would like to simplify the pronunciation of generic and specific names that commemorate peoples' names, both the traditional English devotees and the reformed academics pronounce each vowel and apply the rules of stress set forth in Stearn's *Botanical Latin*. Hence they both pronounce *Acer davidii* as *A. da-VID-ee-eye*, not *A. DAY-vid-eye* as we sometimes hear today. However, as you can see from the pronunciation chart on Page 9 the two sides will not always agree on how the vowels sound.

One more complication to pronouncing botanical names is the gender issue. The gender of the specific epithet matches the gender of the genus, and that gender is not always obvious. Hence, endings such as *folius* will sometimes be *folia* or *folium*. I spent a wonderful day with a very knowledgeable plantsman in England. His solution to remembering the gender-related endings was to simply skim over them without really pronouncing them. Hardly anyone noticed.

I have discovered over the years some "absolutes" in pronouncing botanical names that are really useful: **In names ending in:**

1. *atus, ata, atum*—regardless of the number of syllables, the accent is on the next to last syllable—A-tus, A-ta, A-tum.
    When the *A* is preceded by a consonant, it becomes part of the next to last syllable, hence NA-tus, LA-tus, TA-tus, e-LA-tus, aggre-GA-tus, grandipunc-TA-tus, albomargi-NA-tus.
2. *folius*—regardless of the number of syllables preceding it, the accent is on FOL-ius—ova-li-FOL-ius, pla-ni-FOL-ius, quer-ci-FOL-ius.
3. *florus, flora, florum, the* accent is on the FLO—bi-FLO-rus, grandi-FLO-rus, oppositi-FLO-rus.
4. *phyllus, phylla, phyllum*, the accent is on the next to last syllable—rhizo-FILL-us, glauco-FILL-us, chryso-FILL-um.
5. *phila*, the accent is on the preceding syllable as in Gyp-SO-fi-la.
6. *petalus, petala, petalum*, the accent is on pet—longi-PET-al-us, hexa-PET-al-a.

7. *formis*, the accent is on FORM—con-FORM-is, dif-FORM-is, fili-FORM-is.
8. *anus, ana, anum*, the accent is on the first syllable no matter how many syllables there are—vir-gi-ni-A-na.
9. *ense, ensis* (which is used to denote where a plant comes from), the accent is always on the EN no matter how many syllables—ne-va-DEN-se, mis-sou-ri-EN-sis.

When I conceived of this column, I hoped to discover the "true" pronunciation of botanical Latin, but there really isn't one correct way. I'll leave you with some words of wisdom from William T. Stearn: "How they [botanical Latin names] are pronounced really matters little provided they sound pleasant and are understood by all concerned." I hope having these guidelines will give even the most timid of you the courage to give botanical Latin a try.

Pronunciation Chart

Reformed Academic	Traditional English
ā as in *father*	*fate*
a as in *apart*	*fat*
ae as in ai in *aisle*	as ae in *meat*
au as in *house*	as in aw in *bawl*
c always as in *cat*	{before a, o, u as in *cat*
	{before e, i, y as in *center*
ch (Greek words) as *k*	as *k* or *ch*
ē as in *they*	*me*
e as in *pet*	*pet*
ei as in *rein*	as in *height*
g always as in *go*	{hard before a, o, u as in *gap*
	{soft before e, i, y as in *gem*
ī as in *machine*	*ice*
i as in *pit*	*pit*
j (consonant i) as in *yellow*	j as in *jam*
ng as in *finger*	*finger*
ō as in note	*note*
o as in *not*	*not*
oe as in *oi* in *toil*	as *ee* in *bee*
ph as *p* or *p-h* if possible	like *f*
r always trilled	
s as in *sit, gas*	*sit, gas*
t as in *table*	*table* but ti w/in a word as *nation*
ū as in *brute*	*brute*
u as in *full*	*tub*
ui as *oui* (French), <u>we</u>	*ruin*
v (consonant u) as in *w*	as in *van*
y as u in French *pur*	as in *cypher*
y as in French *du*	as in *cynical*

Stearn, (1992, pp 52-53).

10

Let's Get Started

Colors: Black and White

Help in selecting the right plant for a particular spot in your garden can often be found in the specific name of a plant. I love it when the name tells me something about the color of the plant, its flowers, its leaves, or maybe its fruit. If asked what the Latin for white is, I'm sure all of you would answer ***albus***, ***alba*** or ***album***. And you would be correct. But, as those of us who have ever gone shopping for white paint know, there are many shades of white. Botanical Latin can differentiate some of these shades.

To keep things simple, I'll give only the masculine ending. But you need to remember that the ending of the specific epithet matches the gender of the genetic name. For example:

- A snow white flower would be described by ***niveus*** (NI-vee-us), *nivea* (NI-vee-a) or ***niveum*** (NI-vee-um).
- A pure white flower might be called ***candidus*** (KAN-di-dus) as in *Lilium candidum* (LI-lee-um KAN-di-dum) or *Viburnum farreri* 'Candidissimum' (vye-BUR-num far-RE-ree kan-di-DISS-i-mum).
- A milky-white flower, one which is dull white verging on blue, could bear the name ***lacteus*** (LAK-tee-us) or ***galacto-*** (ga-LAK-toh) if found in a Greek compound word. *Galanthus* (ga-LAN-thus), the snowdrop, gets its name from the Greek ***gala*** (milk).
- Chalk-white could be described by ***cretaceus*** (kre-TAY-see-us), ***calcareus*** (kal-KA-ree-us), *or* ***gypseus*** (JIP-see-us). They all make you think of limestone don't they.
- Silvery white is denoted by ***argenteus*** (ar-JEN-tee-us) as in *Salvia argentea* (SAL-vee-a ar-JEN-tee-a) with the marvelous silver-haired foliage.
- ***Albidus*** (AL-bi-dus), ***albescens*** (al-BES-senz), and ***candicans*** (KAN-di-kans) mean sort of white with ***albidus*** indicating a dirty white and ***albescens*** and ***candicans*** becoming white.
- ***Dealbatus*** (dee-al-BAY-tus) denotes something is whitened, as in a dark back-

ground slightly covered over with white. The bottoms of the leaves of *Centaurea dealbata* (sen-TAW-ree-a dee-al-BAY-ta) look like they are covered with a whitish powder.

The apparent absence of color is indicated by such terms as *aqueus* (A-kwee-us) clear as water, *cyrstallinus* (kri-STAL-li-nus) clear as ice, or *vitreus* (VI-tree-us) glassy.

Then there are the grays.

- Pearl-gray is *griseus* (GRI-see-us) as in *Acer griseum* (ay-ser GRI-see-um) where the underside of the leaf is gray.
- *Cinereus* (si-NE-ree-us) is ash-gray.
- In compounds of Greek words ash-gray is denoted by *tephro-*(TEF-roh) or *spodo* (SPOH-doh).
- Slate and lead are both blue-grays. The Latin for them is *schistaceus* (shis-TAY-cee-us) and *plumbeus* (PLUM-bee-us). Another blue gray which is perhaps a bit duller is described as *lividus (*LI-vi-dus*)*, or *liveus* (LI-vee-us).
- *Canus* (KAY-nus) and *incanus* (in-KAY-nus) indicate a hoary appearance caused by white hairs on the surface of the leaves. *Veronica incana* (ve-RON-i-ka in-KAY-na) with its grey-haired leaves is a good example.

Even black is not an absolute color. Pure black without the mixture of any other color is described in Latin by *ater* (A-ter), *atra* (A-tra), *atrum* (A-trum). When *atro-*(A-troh) is added to a color, it indicates very dark as in *atropurpurea* (a-troh-pur-PUR-ee-a) a very dark purple.

In Greek compound words pure blackness is indicated by the prefixes *mela- (ME-la)* and *melano-* (ME-la-noh) as in *Aronia melanocarpa* (a-ROH-nee-a me-la-noh-KAR-pa) the black fruited chokecherry. Black with a tinge of gray is *niger* (NYE-jer) or *nigrescens* (nye-GRES-sens). *Pinus nigra* (PYE-nus NYE-gra) is the Black Pine.

Ever notice how black some spruce forests look from a distance? Spruce trees get their generic name from the Latin for pitch black, *picea* (correctly pronounced as PYE-see-a but universally pronounced as pye-SEE-a). You get a doubly black tree in *Picea nigra* (PYE-see-a NYE-gra).

That's a black and white look at plant names. Next we'll look at some of the brighter colors.

Warm Colors

Taking my cue from the warm hues of the fall foliage colors, that surround me as I write this column, we'll look this month at the browns, yellows and oranges and reds in plant nomenclature. A quick look at the sections on these colors in Stearns *Botanical Latin* (4th Ed. 1992) offers more shades than any of us will ever remember. But I think the subtlety of description that is possible through these Latin terms is fascinating. Let's look first at the color brown.

- *Brunneus* (BRU-nee-us) is the basic brown.
- A good clear date-brown is described by *spadiceus* (spa-DEE-see-us).
- Add a little red and you might get a chestnut color denoted by both *badius* (BA-dee-us) and *castaneus* (kas-TA-nee-us). *Castanea sativa* (kas-TA-nee-a sa-TEE-va) is the sweet chestnut that street vendors roast at holiday time.
- *Cinnamomeus* (si-na-MOH-mee-us) gives us a cinnamon shade - a bright brown mixed with a little red and yellow.
- A light rusty red is *ferrugineus* (fer-roo-JI-nee-us). With a little more redness you get *rufus* (ROO-fus). Have you ever enjoyed watching a Rufous hummingbird working over your fuchsias? Same color.
- The hazelnut, *Corylus avellana* (KO-ri-lus a-vel-LAY-na), gives us the hazel color of *corylinus* (ko-ri-LYE-nus).
- Then there are the dirty browns like *fuliginosus* (fu-li-ji-NOH-sus) a sooty brown verging on black and *luridus* (LUR-i-dus) a dirty clouded brown.

Before we all get depressed by the drabness of browns, let's move into the bright colors of yellow. What shades of yellow come readily to mind?

- The purest yellow might be lemon denoted by *citreus* (SIT-ree-us) or *citrinus* (si-TRY-nus).
- Then there is gold, a pure color but duller than lemon. It is denoted by *aureus* (AU-ree-us) or *auratus* (au-RAY-tus).
- In Greek composite words you will see *chryso-* (KRIS-oh) as in *Chrysanthemum* (kris-AN-the-mum) or *Chrysogonum* (kris-O-goh-num).

- A clear yellow without any tinges of orange or green or brown is *luteus* (LOO-tee-us) while a paler clear yellow is *flavus* (FLAY-vus). The airy pale yellow flowers of the yellow meadow rue, *Thalictrum flavum glaucum,* (tha-LIK-trum FLAY-vum GLAU-kum) come to mind.
- Other pale yellows can be *luteolus* (loo-tee-OH-lus), *lutescens* loo-TES-senz) or *flavididus* (FLAY-vi-dus).
- In Greek compound words this color is depicted as *xanthus* (ZAN-thus) as in *xanthoceras* (zan-THO-se-ras) a shrub in the rose family which has yellow horn-like appendages between the petals. *Keras* is Greek for horn.

  Yellows shaded with other colors give us some interesting names:
- sulphur-colored-*sulphureus* (sul-FEUR-ee-us);
- straw-colored *stramineus* (stra-MI-nee-us),
- orange-yellow – *auranticaus* (au-ran-tee-AH-kus),
- tawny or buff – *fulvus* (FUL-vus) and
- livid (clouded with grey, brown or blue hints) - *lividus* (LI-vi-dus).
- A pure strong orange is described as *aurantius* (au-RAN-tee-us).
- *Cupreus* (KOO-pree-us) and *cuprescens* (koo-PRES-senz) describe a copper color,
- while *croceus* (KROH-see-us) denotes the rich orange of saffron that comes from the bright orange pollen of *Crocus sativa* (KROH-kus sa-TEE-va).

   The line between yellow-orange, orange, red-orange, and brownish-red is often hard difficult to pin down. Hence, we see some crossover of terms for red and orange. For instance, *ferrugineus* can be listed as a rusty brown shade, an orange shade or even a reddish-brown shade. The same is true of *rubiginosus* (roo-bi-ji-NOH-sus) or *rufus* (ROO-fus) In the end it doesn't matter whether we list them today in the brown-yellow-orange group or in the red group. All we need to do is remember they mean rust-colored.

   Other terms that describe red shades include:
- *Ruber* (ROO-ber) is true red and it gives us *rubri-* (ROO-bri) in compound words and the various forms of *rubescens (*roo-BES-senz*)* and *rubellus* (roo-BEL-us) pale or becoming red, *rubeus* (ROO-bee-us), and *rubicundus* (roo-bi-KUN-dus).
- Terms for carmine red include *carmineus* (kar-MI-nee-us), and *coccineus* (kok-SI-nee-us). *Puniceus* (pu-NEE-see-us) is crimson while *phoeniceus* (foh-

NEE-see-us) is scarlet.

- Rosy is depicted by *roseus* (ROH-zee-us) and *rhodo-* (ROH-doh) in Greek compound words. *Rhododendron* literally means rose tree.
- Shadings of red include purple-red - *purpureus* (pur-PUR-ee-us); dull red - *sanguineus* (san-GWI-nee-us); flame-red - *flammeus* (FLA-mee-us) or *igneus* (IG-nee-us); and **vermilion** (scarlet with a hint of yellow) - *miniatus* (mi-nee-AY-tus) or *vermiculatus* (ver-mi-kew-LAY-tus). Coral-red is, naturally, *corallinus* (ko-ral-LYE-nus).

As you can see, there is no shortage of descriptive terms for red or any of the various shades of fall foliage. Some of these terms are probably familiar to you. Even if you don't remember the exact shading of one of these terms the next time you come upon it, perhaps you will remember that the color is one of the reds or browns or oranges or yellows. And that is something.

Cool Colors

In a lecture I found particularly interesting, Richard Hartlage talked about the different values for colors and demonstrated visually what Latin nomenclature is trying to describe verbally. In this final discussion of color words we'll take a look at the greens, blues, and purples and then wind up with some terms for color variegations and markings.

The most commonly used term for green is *viridus* (VI-ri-dus). When used in compound words it becomes:

- *viridiflorus* (vi-ri-di-FLO-rus), having green flowers,
- *viridifolius* (vi-ri-di-FOL-ee-us), having green leaves, or maybe
- *viridissimus* (vi-ri-DIS-si-mus), very green or greenest.

Virens (VI-renz) is another word for green. The coastal redwood is *Sequoia sempervirens* (see-KWOY-a sem-per-VI-renz) or evergreen sequoia. Pure green in Greek compound words is represented by *chloro-* (KLOR-o) as in *Chlorophora* (klor-OF-or-a) a plant that produces green dye.

Seagreen is often described by *glaucus* (GLAU-kus) or *glaucescens* (glau-KES-senz) because of the "bloom" or white powdery appearance that makes green seem blue-green.

Moving to a very dark green, one with a touch of black, the name might be *atrovirens* (a-TRO-vi-renz).

Pure blue is *caeruleus* (se-REW-lee-us) in Latin or *cyaneus* (sy-AN-ee-us) from the Greek *kyanos*. These are the two most often seen in plant names.

There are, however, some other shades of blue.

- Indigo (deep blue) is *indigoticus* (in-di-GO-ti-kus),
- sky-blue is *azureus* (a-ZU-ree-us),
- lavender (pale blue with some grey added) is *caesius* (SE-see-us),
- violet (pure blue stained with red) is *violaceus* (vye-oh-LAY-see-us), and
- lilac (pale, dull violet with a little white) is *lilacinus* (lye-LA-si-nus).

We have already discussed some of the shades of purple in our section on red hues. A few others you might run into are:

19

ethystinus (a-me-this-TYE-nus) the violet color of the stone, *hyacinthinus* (high-a-sin-THI-nus) a deep purplish-blue, and *vinosus* (vi-NOH-sus) wine colored.

Before we leave the discussion of color in plant names, there is one more area that deserves mention *i.e.,* variegation and color markings. I doubt anyone would have trouble with visualizing something named *variegatus* (va-ree-e-GAY-tus). Strictly speaking the term refers to irregular colors in sinuous spaces. Often the color of the variegation is added to the name as in *aureovariegatus* (au-ree-o-va-ree-e-GAY-tus) having gold or yellow variegation.

- Blotches of color are described by *maculatus* (mak-yew-LAY-tus).
- The term for spots or speckles of color is *guttatus* (gut-TAY-tus).
- The one for round dots of color is *punctaus* (punk-TAY-tus).
- When one color is bordered by another, we use *limbatus* (lim-BAY-tus).
- When narrowly edged by a color, we use *marginatus* (mar-ji-NAY-tus).
- When colors are spread in streaks of unequal intensity, the term is *pictus (PIK-tus)* for painted.

Some terms imply color without being specific. *Pictus, variegatus, punctatus,* and *guttatus* can be used this way. Others are words like *coloratus* (ko-lor-AY-tus), *concolor* (KON-ko-lor), *bicolor* (BYE-ko-lor), and *mutabilis* (mew-TA-bi-lis) which literally means changeable in color.

Has this review of color terms helped you think about color in the garden as well as in plant names? It certainly colored my thinking.

I was struck by an observation pertaining to color over several fall seasons. It changes every year. One year I photographed a lot of fall leaves looking for a photograph to enter in a flower show. The next fall I could hardly wait for the same "photo ops" to happen again. To my surprise, they didn't. Although there was probably more color overall the second fall than the first, the same trees I had photographed the first year weren't as striking the second, while others were much better. I also noticed in my own garden that this year the *Fothergilla gardenii* 'Jane Platt' and the deciduous azalea *Rhododendron luteum* made fabulous red leaves at the same time! This display has not happened for a number of years, although I hope for it every year. For all of my planning and planting, in the end, nature has a way of deciding the final colorscape each year. Maybe that's what keeps me interested in and challenged by my garden and year after year.

Inflorescence: Flowers in Groups

A friend asked me the other day what the white-flowered trees were that are blooming all around town. When I asked her to describe the flowers, she was pretty vague, so a firm answer from me was difficult. Had she known the specific terms for the various types of flowers that give a visual picture of the inflorescence, my response would have been easier.

Some plants have single flowers on a stem, but a great many more plants have groups of flowers in particular arrangements on their stems. These grouped flowers form an *inflorescence* which can take many forms. It might be a spike, a raceme, a cyme, a panicle, an umbel, a spadix, or a corymb, to name the most common forms. Sometimes the type of inflorescence gives the species its botanical name. Let's look at the some of the different types of inflorescence and the Latin names derived from them.

The Latin *spicatus* (spi-KAY-tus) denotes a **spike** inflorescence. That means the individual flowers are stalkless or *sessile*, and are arranged along the axis or *peduncle*. Although *Veronica spicata* (ve-RON-i-ka spi-KAY-ta) comes quickly to mind as representing the spike form, a willow's catkin and the worm-like flowers of a birch tree are also specialized forms of spikes.

Spike

A **raceme**, from which we get such specific names as *racemosa* (ray-si-MOH-sa), is a modified spike in that the flowers have stalks (pedicels) that attach to the peduncle. Wisteria is a good example. Some of you may have *Cimicifuga racemosa* (si-mi-si-FEW-ga ray-si-MOH-sa), a summer bloomer, or *C. simplex* (SIM-plex) the fall flowering species in

Raceme

your gardens These are another example of raceme inflorescence. (Note: When you discuss a number of species of the same genus in a list, as I've done here, you can abbreviate the name of the genus with a capital letter. This is common practice in catalogs and reference books.)

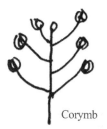

Corymb

The terms **corymb** and **umbel** have always confused me. They are much alike in that they both have clusters of flowers attached to the peduncle by pedicels or stalks and they both bloom from the outside toward the center. However, in a **corymb** the flower pedicels attach at <u>different</u> points along the peduncle like cherry and apple blossoms. In an **umbel**, the flowers are connected at the <u>same</u> point on the peduncle like "Queen Anne's lace." Latin names derived from these forms are *umbellatus* (um-bel-LAY-us), *corymbifer* (KORYM-bi-fer), and *corymbosus* (korym-BOH-sus).

Umbel

You see many references to a **cyme** inflorescence when you read about viburnums. A **cyme** is a flat or convex inflorescence in which the inner flowers open first. Zonal geraniums, phlox, and dogwood species are good examples in addition to viburnums.

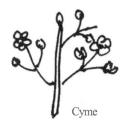

Cyme

A **panicle** is a complex inflorescence with repeated branching. It can be made up of many **racemes, spikes, corymbs, cymes** or **umbels**. *Pieris* (PYE-er-is) is a good example of racemose-panicles; corn an example of spikose-panicles; *Pyracantha* (pye-ra-KAN-tha) of corymbose-panicles; and *Aralia* (a-RAY-lee-a) of umbellose-panicles. When you see *paniculata* (pa-nik-yew-LAY-ta) as the specific name, you can be certain the flowers will be numerous and in bunches.

Panicle
(of Racemes)

Members of the *Araceae* (air-AY-see-ee) or Arum family have a **spadix** form of inflorescence. A spadix is spike-like with tiny, sessile (stemless) flowers. It is generally enclosed in a spathe.

If you can keep a picture in your mind of a raceme, an umbel, a corymb, a spike or spadix in your mind, you should have some idea of the plant's flowers when you see *racemosa, umbellata, corymbosa* or *spicata*. It should also help you identify plants when there is a time lapse between seeing the plant in someone's garden and looking it up in your book.

Spadix

Spathe

A couple of other flower-related Latin names can also be helpful.

- *grandiflora* (gran-di-FLO-ra) indicates a plant makes large or showy flowers
- *floribunda* (flo-ri-BUN-da) that a plant makes lots of flowers; and
- *flora pleno* (FLO-ra PLAY-noh) that a plant has double flowers.

If a picture is worth a thousand words, these pictures should be worth many many plant names.

Flowers Individually

We have talked about the arrangement of flowers into spikes, racemes, corymbs, umbels, etc., but we have not discussed the individual flowers themselves. So let's take a closer look at individual flowers that either make up an inflorescence or stand alone as solitary flowers. There is much to be learned from the flowers of a plant because most of the science which classifies plants relates to the flower parts.

Flowers are the sexual organs of plants and are responsible for plant reproduction. Typically we look first at the colorful petals which serve to lure the necessary pollinator to the reproductive organs. However, the male organ or **stamen,** made up of the **filament** (stalk) and the **anther**, which holds the pollen, and the female organ or **pistil,** made up of the **ovary**, the **style** (stalk) and the **stigma** (the pollen receptacle) are the necessary parts of any flower.

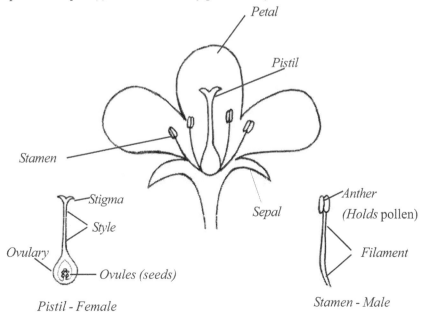

Petal

Pistil

Stamen

Stigma

Style

Ovulary

Ovules (seeds)

Sepal

Anther
(Holds pollen)

Filament

Pistil - Female

Stamen - Male

The basic flower parts are essentially the same, but appear in an almost infinite variety of ways. For example, the ovary - made up of the ovulary (container) and the ovules (seeds within the ovulary) can be situated above the petals (superior), below the petals (inferior), or in a cup-like vessel inside the petals (hypanthium).

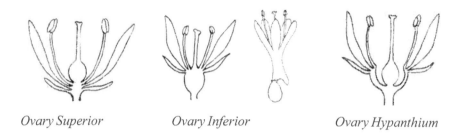

Ovary Superior   *Ovary Inferior*   *Ovary Hypanthium*

The various arrangements of the sexual parts are important if you are trying to identify a plant. But for most of us, it is the arrangement and form of the petals that engage us. The collected petals form the **corolla** and it is the corolla which creates the flower shapes we recognize. Some of the most common corolla forms are shown below.

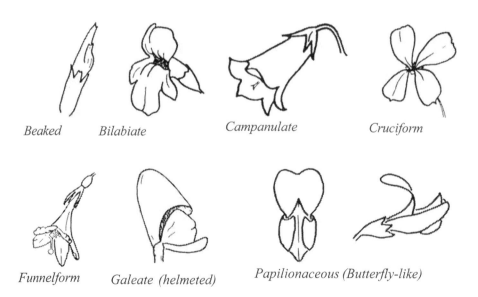

Beaked   *Bilabiate*   *Campanulate*   *Cruciform*

Funnelform   *Galeate (helmeted)*   *Papilionaceous (Butterfly-like)*

Corolla forms continued:

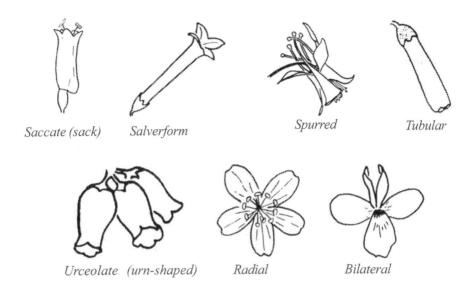

Saccate (sack)   Salverform   Spurred   Tubular

Urceolate (urn-shaped)   Radial   Bilateral

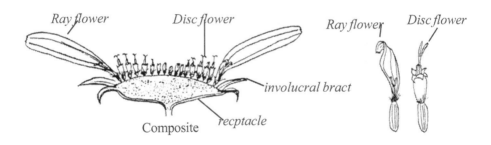

Ray flower   Disc flower   Ray flower   Disc flower

involucral bract

Composite   recptacle

Plant families are made up of a groups of genera which share common traits. Their flowers are key to their placement in a particular plant family. So I hope this introduction to flowers and their parts will be helpful to you. A discussion of flower parts and the sexlife of plants can get very scientific and overhwleming. Hopefully, this little bit of information will help you with both your use of botanical Latin and also with your enjoyment of plants.

Berries and Other Fruit

Among my favorite things in a winter garden are berries that add color to an otherwise drab landscape. The fruits of the *Rosaceae* (rohz-AY-see-ee) or Rose Family are a good place to start.

My job would be a breeze if all the members of the *Rosaceae* had the same kind of fruit, but they don't. Actually there are four distinct types of fruit and a couple of variations of some of those. When I've tried to write a column about fruits before, I've given up because the subject matter isn't easily simplified and it doesn't fit the typical *Fearless Latin* format. However, I'll try to present it so that we can all get a grasp on fruits.

Let's start with the fruit of the genus *Rosa* (ROH-za). Rose hips are not, as I have long thought, funny little apples. So I've learned something right off the bat. A **hip** is actually a fleshy container which is developed from the floral cup and which encloses the *achenes*. What is an **achene**? It is a dry, indehiscent fruit with a thin, tight outer wall.

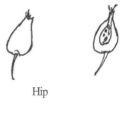

Hip

Since we'll see the terms "dehiscent" and "indehiscent" frequently, let's define each right now. If a fruit is "dehiscent," it splits along definite lines when ripe. A pea pod is dehiscent. The opposite is "indehiscent." There are no lines around the fruit along which it can open when ripe.

There are many types of achenes some of which have prominent *styles* which provide a mode of travel for the seed. A good example of an achene of this type, but one that is not from the rose family, is a dandelion,

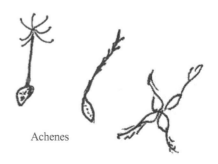

Achenes

Taraxacum officinale (ta-RAX-a-kum oh-fi-si-NA-lee). The fruit is attached to the feathery style which allows it to be borne on the wind. In the *Rosaceae* a good example is the feathery achene of *Dryas octopetala* (DRY-as c-toh-PE-ta-la) the Mountain avens.

Not all achenes have feathery styles, however. A staple of our grandmothers' gardens was *Rhodotypos scandens* (roh-doh-TYE-pohz SKAN-denz) commonly called jetbead. Its fruits are small black beads that are quite dry, very hard, have no circumferential lines (indehiscent) and contain a single seed.

There is yet another kind of achene fruit, called an **accessory fruit**. A good example is the strawberry, *Fragaria* sp. (fra-GA-ree-a) which embeds its achenes on the outside of its fleshy fruit.

Accessory fruit

One other achene fruit I should mention is the burr like that of *Acaena* (a-SEE-na), the New Zealand burr. Its name comes from the Greek *akaina* meaning thorn and alludes to the spines on the calyx. The burrs of this plant attach themselves to anything walking by.

Another common fruit type in the *Rosaceae* is the **pome**. The name comes from *Pomum,* the Latin for apple. Apples, pears, quince, flowering quince and hawthorns are perfect examples. A pome is a fleshy fruit that has several *locules* (chambers or cavities). It is formed from the fusion of the interior ovary with the *hypanthium* (the cup-like structure formed by the basal portions of the calyx, corolla, and stamens) also called the floral cup. Just so you won't feel you are missing your Latin this month, here are the names of the genera exemplifying a pome. The genus for:

Pome

- apples is *Malus* (MA-lus);
- pears *Pyrus (PEER-us);*
- quince *Cydonia* (si-DOH-nee-a);
- flowering or Japanese quince *Chaenomeles* (key-NOM-el-eez); and
- hawthorn *Crataegus* (kra-TEE-jus).

30

If you see a plant with the specific epithet ***pomifera*** (pom-IF-er-a), you can be pretty certain its fruit resembles an apple.

Cherries, plums, peaches and apricots are members of the genus *Prunus* (PREW-nus) and form another type of fruit called a **drupe**. A drupe is a stone fruit, which means it is an indehiscent fruit with a single seed (usually) enclosed in a stony case that is in turn enclosed in the fleshy or fibrous outer layers. (The stony case is called an endocarp which literally means the inner seed.) Picture a peach pit and you have it. Our Oregon native *Oemleria cerasiformis* (eem-LER-ee-a se-ras-si-FORM-iss), or Indian plum, has a small drupe-type fruit. *Oemleria,* by the way, honors Augustus Oemler a German-born naturalist. *Cerasus* is Latin for cherry so the specific epithet alludes to the cherry-like fruit. ***Cerasifer*** (si-RA-sif-er) could be the name for a plant bearing cherry-like fruit while ***cerasinus*** (si-RAS-in-us) indicates a cherry-red color.

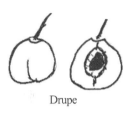

Drupe

Not all stone fruits are as obvious as cherries and plums, however. Brambles like raspberries, black-berries and others in the genus *Rubus* (ROO-bus) have **aggregate fruits** made up of multiple drupes. These are produced by a single flower and borne on a common receptacle - in this case the fleshy fruit.

Aggregate fruit

The last type of fruit found in the rose family is the **follicle**. To be perfectly honest I'm not sure I've ever seen the follicular fruits of the rose family. Some of the genera that bear follicular fruits are *Aruncus* (a-RUN-kus), *Neillia* (NIEL-lee-a) *Physocarpus* (fye-soh-KARP-us) and *Spiraea* (spy-REE-a). All of these have clusters of small flowers and, apparently, small seeds as well. By definition, a follicle is a dry, dehis-cent fruit with one to many seeds derived from a single carpel. It splits along the inner or ventral side of the fruit when ripe. I'll have to pay more attention to my *Neillia et al* next year to see if I can see the follicles.

Follicle

I started this column saying I loved the berries in winter. But we have just seen that many fruits we think of as "berries" are really drupes, aggregate or accessory fruits, or small pomes like those of *Cotoneaster* (koh-toh-nee-AS-ter). That includes not only members of the rose family but also members of the holly family as well. So what is a **true berry**? By definition it is a juicy, indehiscent fruit, with one to many seeds, which is the product of a single pistil. Here are a few examples.

True berry

In the *Caprifoliaceae* (kap-ri-foh-lee-AY-see-e) the fruits of *Lonicera* (lon-NISS-er-a), or honeysuckle, are true berries as are those of our native snowberry, *Symphoricarpos albus* (sim-for-i-KARP-ozs AL-bus). The natal plum, *Carissa grandiflora* (ka-RISS-a gran-di-FLO-ra), a member of the *Apocynaceae* (a-po-si-NAY-see-ee) or dogbane family that you see in warmer climes, is also a berry. So, incidentally, are some members of the *Solanaceae* (soh-la-NAY-see-ee) or nightshade family like *Capsicum* (KAP-si-kum), peppers both sweet and hot, and *Solanum melongena* (soh-LAN-um me-lo-noh-JEE-na) the eggplant. I don't know about you, but I never thought of eggplant as being a berry! I guess we had better be careful when writing fall flower show schedules to use the words "fruited branches" rather than "berried branches."

I hope you stuck with me through the dry definitions and have come to better understand the numerous types of fruit in the garden. *Hortus Third* gives the type of fruit each genus produces in the general description for each genus. You will probably find some more interesting surprises like eggplant berries.

Hairy Things

Here is a quick quiz for you. What do *Tricyrtis hirta* (try-SIR-tus HIR-ta), *Pterostyrax hispidus* (te-roh-STY-rax HIS-pi-dus), *Rhododendron strigillosum* (R. stri- ji-LOH-sum) and *Eriophyllum lanatum* (Air-ee-O-fil-lum la-NAY-tum) have in common? The answer is that they are all hairy. Since the presence (or sometimes the absence) of hairs on a plant can be a distinguishing characteristic of the plant, it is often reflected in the plant's name.

There are a number of different kinds of hairiness. Some plants are woolly, some are bristly, while others are silky, velvety, or downy. To keep the things simple, I will, once again, give only the masculine form for the Latin words. But keep in mind that the gender of a Latin specific epithet reflects the gender of the generic name. That means you'll find these descriptive terms ending in the masculine *-us,* the feminine *-a*, or the neuter *-um.*

The term **pubescent** is generally used to mean a plant is covered with hairs. Strictly speaking, however, it indicates a covering of soft, fine or downy hairs. Several forms of this term include:

- *pubens* (POO-benz)
- *pubescens* (poo-BESS-senz)
- *pubiger* (POO-bi-jer)

Other terms that indicate downiness and sample specific usages are:

- *pilosus,* (pi-LOH-sus)—**pilose:** covered, but not densely so, with fine, soft, straight hairs
- *villosus* (vi-LOH-sus)—**villose:** covered with long, shaggy, unmatted hairs
- *sericeus* (se-RI-see-us) or *sericifer* (se-RI-si-fer)—**sericeous:** covered with silky, soft, fine, appressed hairs
- *velutinus* (ve-lew-TYE-nus)—**velutinous:** covered with velvety, erect, straight and moderately firm hairs

The presence of woolly hairs is described by such terms as:

- *tomentosus*, (toh-men-TOH-sus)— **tomentose:** having densely matted, short, woolly hairs
- *lanatus* (la-NAY-tus), *laniger* (LAN-i-jer), or *lanosus* (la-NOH-sus)— **lanate:** bearing long, intertwined, woolly hairs
- *lanuginosus,* (la-new-ji-NOH-sus)—**lanuginose:** bearing woolly hairs shorter than lanate

The last group of hairy plants are those with bristles or bristly hairs. They are identified as:

- *hirsutus* (hir-SOO-tus), *hirtus* (HIR-tus), or *hirtellus* (hir-TEL-lus)—**hirsute:** with coarse, stiff hairs
- *hispidus* (HIS-pi-dus)—**hispid:** beset with bristles
- *setosus* (se-TOH-sus), *setaceus* (se-TAY-see-us)—**setose:** covered with bristles
- *strigosus* (stri-GOH-sus), *strigillosus* (stri-ji-LOH-sus)—**strigose:** covered with fine, sharp, straight hairs

There are Latin prefixes that also indicate hairiness. The prefixes *tricho-* and *seti-* denote bristly hairs, and the prefix *eri-* affixed to a compound word indicates woolly hairs. Some examples of their usage are::

- *trichosanthus* (tri-koh-SAN-thus) meaning bristly-flowered,
- *setifolius* (se-ti-FOL-ee-us) meaning bristly-leaved, or
- *eriophyllum* (air-ee-o-FILL-lum) meaning woolly-leaved.

The lack of hair can be as distinguishing as its presence and an important clue to identification. The term most often used to denote hairlessness is **glabrous**, with such specific terms as:

- *glabrescens* (gla-BRE-senz)
- *glaber* (GLA-ber)
- *glabellus* (gla-BEL-us)

Although we have divided these "hairy" terms into downy, woolly and bristly following the definitions found in *Hortus Third* and *Stearn's Dictionary of Plant Names for Gardeners*, in the "real world" of plant names the differences are sometimes fuzzy, if you'll excuse the bad pun. One person's "woolly" may be another's "downy." But now, hopefully, the terms pubescent, pilose, glabrous, among others, have meaning for you.

By the way, *Tricyrtis hirta* is a toad lily (terrible name for a pretty plant); *Pterostyrax hispidus* is the epaulet tree; *Eriophyllum lanatum* is our own wonderful yellow wildflower commonly called "Oregon Sunshine", and *Rhododendron strigillosum* is a rhododendron species which has long stiff bristles on its branches, long skinny leaves and scarlet flowers.

Fragrance

Coming upon a fragrant plant while wandering through a garden is one of those lovely things that I never tire of experiencing. It adds a another dimension, stimulates another sense, and creates a mood. Of course, coming upon a malodorous plant can be an experience of a totally different sort. Which illustrates that differences exist in the realm of "smelly" plants. According to the dictionary, fragrance connotes a sweet smell, while scent means a thing possesses a distinctive (but not necessarily sweet) odor or perfume. When it comes to Latin terms various distinctions are made.

There are a number of terms that denote a sweet fragrance. They include, not surprisingly, *aromaticus* (a-roh-MA-ti-kus); *fragrans* (FRAY-granz) and the superlative form, *fragrantissimus* (fray-gran-TISS-si-mus) as well as the various forms of the Latin root *odor*: *odorus* (oh-DOH-rus), *odoratus* (oh-do-RAY-tus), *odorifer* (oh-do-RI-fer) and *odoratissimus* (oh-doh-ra-TISS-simus).

The fragrance of *Daphne odora* (DAFF-nee oh-DOH-ra) wafting on the breeze is a sure sign of spring to me. One of the parents of *Viburnum x bodnantense* (vye-BUR-num x bod-nant-EN-se), the wonderful winter-flowering pink viburnum, is now called *V. farreri* (fa-RA-ree) after Reginald John Farrer (1880-1920), but you will still find it listed as *V. fragrans* (FRAY-grans) in older books. There are some mature white-flowered specimens along the spring walk at Elk Rock Garden of a selection of this Chinese species called 'Candidissimum.'

In your spice cabinet you probably have nutmeg and mace. These both come from the same plant, an evergreen tree that grows in Indonesia called *Myristica fragrans* (mir-IS-ti-ka). Nutmeg is the seed and mace is made from the fibrous seed cover. *Myristica* comes from the Greek *myristikos*, meaning fit for anointing. Once upon a time you might have had oil of wintergreen in your bathroom cabinet or certainly you have chewed wintergreen-flavored gum. The oil comes from *Gaultheria fragrantissima* (gaul-THE-ree-a) which was named for a

Dr. Gaulthier, a Canadian botanist (c. 1708-58).

Another term denoting a sweet scent is ***suaveolens*** (swah-VEE-oh-lens), which comes from the Latin *suavis* meaning delightful. A mint native to Europe with foliage that smells like apples is *Mentha suaveolens* (MEN-tha). Like many of its genus, apple mint is a vigorous perennial with pink and white tubular flowers in the summer. There is a lovely poppy from the Pyrenees Mountains called *Papaver suaveolens* (pa-PAY-ver). I presume it has fragrant flowers or leaves. It is the leaves which are pungently fragrant on *Hakea suaveolens* (HA-kee-a), a member of the Protea family from Australia. *Hakea* is named for a German patron of botany, Baron Ludwig von Hake (1745-1818). This particular *Hakea* is a four- to six-foot shrub with creamy flowers in dense racemes. *Acacia suaveolens* (a-KAY-see-a) is known as the Sweet wattle of eastern Australia.

Those of you with herb gardens are probably acquainted with *Ruta graveolens* (ROO-ta gra-VEE-oh-lenz) or common rue. ***Graveolens*** is another name meaning heavy- or strong-scented. It is a member of the *Rutaceae* or Rue family in which we also find the citrus fruits. The name comes from the Latin word for bitterness or unpleasantness. The flowers of many members of the family smell very sweet so perhaps the bitterness comes from the skin of the fruit. Common dill, which most certainly is strongly-scented is *Anethum graveolens* (a-NEE-thum). A shrub, commonly called Mexican oregano for its aromatic leaves, is *Lippia graveolens* (LIP-pee-a), which was named for Italian naturalist, Augustin Lippi (1678-1701). A member of the Verbena family, the weedy herb Lemon verbena is also a *Lippia* species.

There are names for things that smell bad as well. One we see most commonly is ***foetidus*** (FE-ti-dus) or the superlative, ***foetidissimus*** (fe-ti-DISS-si-mus). *Rosa foetida* is commonly known as the Austrian briar or the Austrian yellow rose. It is the single yellow flowers of this upright shrub that are pungently scented. Many of you probably have the tall, evergreen hellebore, *Helleborus foetidus* (hel-LE-bor-us FE-ti-dus), in your gardens which has an unpleasant order when crushed. You may also cherish the wonderful red-orange seeds that make *Iris foetidissima* (EYE-ris fe-ti-DISS-si-ma) so outstanding. This is an evergreen iris that produces sort of greyish-yellow blooms in early summer. While the flowers are perhaps nondescript, the seeds when they pop from the pod in the fall are very special.

Although I've never really noticed that the smell of either the hellebore or the iris was particularly offensive, I might approach with care of any plant with the specific name of *capreus* (KAP-re-us) or *hircinus* (hir-SYE-nus). Both of them mean to smell like a goat. Having said that, we had a *Salix caprea* 'Pendula' (SAY-lix), now called 'Kilmarnock,' at Elk Rock until a few years ago. Grown as a standard, it made wonderful catkins in the spring. I don't remember a peculiar scent to this goat willow.

Yet another group of Latin names denotes a particular kind of scent or fragrance. For example, *moschatus* (mos-KA-tus) indicates a musky smell. The small, late-blooming yellow monkey flower native to boggy areas in our region is *Mimulus moschatus* (MI-mew-lus), and in tropical Asia there is a tall shrubby perennial with hibiscus-like flowers called *Abelmoschus moschatus* (a-bel-MOS-kus). The name apparently comes from Arabic meaning the father of musk and refers to the smell of the seeds. The well-known Musk rose is *Rosa moschata.* From western Asia, this tall rose (to 10 feet) bears single to semi-double white, musk-scented flowers on lax stems. The flowers are followed by orange hips in the fall.

Caryophyllus, (ka-ree-oh-FIL-lus) suggests the fragrance of clove. The name comes from the hickory tree (*Carya*) whose leaves smell of cloves when crushed. *Dianthus caryophyllus* (dye-AN-thus), commonly called Wild carnation and noted for its strong clove scent, is native to the Mediterranean region. It has been bred and selected for many years to create numerous cultivars many of which have lost the famous fragrance. The family to which *Dianthus* belongs is called the *Caryophyllaceae* (ka-ree-oh-fil-LAY-see-ee) or the family of plants that smell like hickory leaves. Included are such annuals and perennials as the sandworts, *Arenaria* (a-re-NA-ree-a), whose name comes from the Latin *arena* meaning sand; the mouse-ears or chickweeds, *Cerastium* (se-RAS-tee-um), which gets its name from the Greek word *keras* meaning horn for the shape of the seed capsule, *Gypsophila* (jip-SOF-i-la), our baby's breath that gets its name from the gypsum soil it prefers, and the campions, *Silene* (sye-LEE-nee) which get their name from the Greek name for a related plant.

An interesting discovery I made recently is that the spice clove was once classified as *Caryophyllus aromaticus* (a-roh-MA-ti-kus). I suspect its name gave rise to the *Caryophyllaceae.* What is interesting is that the genus *Caryophyllus* is no longer listed in the RHS Dictionary. The clove is now classified as *Syzygium aromaticum*. (I'm guessing the genus is pronounced si-ZI-jee-um.) From the Greek *syzygos,* it means joined and refers to leaf arrangement. Even more interesting is that the clove is not a member of the *Caryophyllaceae* but rather is placed in the Myrtle family or *Myrtaceae* (mer-TAY-see-ee). This seems to be a gap in the scientific order, but we can choose not to worry about it.

As you can see, there are numerous ways to describe the fragrance, scent, smell, or aroma associated with plants. Now use your botanical Latin to help you find fragrant plants for your garden.

Latin Root Words for Plant Parts

In the course of writing these columns, I've spent a great deal of time reading through botanical dictionaries (which are not as dull as you might think) and I've come to a conclusion. Armed with a list of plant parts and a list of frequently-used descriptive prefixes, you can understand a lot of botanical Latin.

In previous columns, we've seen specific names which are actually compound words describing a characteristic of some part of the plant that makes it distinct from other members of its genus. Up to now in our discussions, the plant parts themselves have been secondary to the descriptive words indicating color or shape. This time, I thought we'd take a look at 30 often-used root words indicating plant parts. By now some of them should be old friends to you, and this list won't be overwhelming. I've shown only the masculine form of each word, but you will see these same roots ending in the feminine "*a*" and neuter "*um*" as well.

-a-CAN-thus - spines

-AN-drus - stamen

-AN-thus, -AN-the-mos - flower

-an-gu-LA-ris - angle

-BO-trys - cluster

-CAR-pus - fruit

-cau-DA-tus - tail

-CAU-lis - stem

-CEPH-a-lus - head

-CLA-dus - branch

-COR-nis - horn

-den-TA-tis, dens - tooth

-FI-dus - cleft

-FLO-rus - flower

-FOL-i-us - leaf

-GLOS-sus - tongue

-LEP-is - scale

-LO-bus, -lo-BA-tus - lobe

-NER-vis - vein

-o-DO-nis - tooth

-pes, -PO-dus - foot, stalk

-PET-a-lus - petal

-PHYL-us - leaf

-pter (**ter**) - wings

-RYE-zus - root

-SEP-a-lus - sepal

-STE-mon - stamen

STACH-yus - spike

To illustrate how these roots are used, let me give you an example. These roots can be combined with a numerical prefix. If we add the prefix "*bi*," meaning two of something, to any of the words below, see what happens. We get **bidens** (two-toothed), **bifolius** (two-leaved), **bicornis** (two-horned), **biflorus** (two-flowered), and so on.

Once these words are stored in your memory banks, you'll have access to hundreds of plant names. You've already stored many descriptive modifiers for these root words in the form of colors, leaf shapes, and the like.

Now we need to add some commonly-used prefixes which, when added to these roots, will help you decipher many more botanical names. Just for fun I have a little game for you to challenge your memory banks. All the words have appeared in previous chapters. Have fun.

Fearless Latin Matching Game

____	1. angustifolius	A. hairless
____	2. caryophyllus	B. clove scented
____	3. chrysocarpus	C. bristled
____	4. cordifolius	D. sweet smelling
____	5. cyananthus	E. kidney shaped
____	6. floribundus	F. covered with short, dense hairs
____	7. foetidissimus	G. spatula shaped
____	8. glaber	H. many flowered
____	9. grandiflorus	I. showy flowered
____	10 hispidus	J. narrow leaved
____	11. lanatus	K. blue flowered
____	12. nigripes	L. shield shaped
____	13. peltatus	M. covered with shaggy airs
____	14. reniformis	N. hairy flowered
____	15. rubronervis	O. yellow fruited
____	16. spatulatus	P. heart shaped leaves
____	17. suaveolens	Q. foul smelling
____	18. tomentosus	R. blacked stalked
____	19. trichosanthus	S. red veined
____	20. villosus	T. woolly

Answers

1J, 2B, 3O, 4P, 5K, 6H, 7Q, 8A, 9I, 10C, 11T, 12R, 13L, 14E, 15S, 16G, 17D, 18F, 19N, 20M

Helpful Prefixes

I hope you didn't find that list of botanical plant parts too difficult digest, and that you are ready to add a list of common botanical prefixes to go with them. Lists can be intimidating. I still remember the spelling test, of some 100 or more words, we had to take at the beginning and end of every year in elementary school. Each year we learned a few more words and, by the end of the 6th grade, we had to spell them all correctly. I think the real lesson was that repetition is a good thing. If you study something often enough, you'll begin to remember it. Little by little you add pieces to your memory. A similar approach works for botanical Latin.

After much thought about how best to organize this list of prefixes, I finally decided that alphabetically was probably the simplest way, if not the most creative. I've also added a few examples of each to show how they are used.

a - lacking, contrary to,
  a-CAU-lis - stemless
  a-PE-ta-lus - without petals
acanth- spiny, thorny
  a-can-tho-CAR-pus - with spiny fruit
acu - sharply pointed
  a-cu-mi-na-ti-FOL-i-us - leaves tapering to long points
  a-cu-ti-LO-bus - having sharply pointed lobes
aden - having glands
  a-de-NOPH-orus - having glands
  a-den-o-PHYL-lus - leaves are sticky from glands
atro - dark
  a-tro-KAR-pus - with dark fruit

a-tro-CAU-lis - with dark stems
chamae - dwarf or low-growing
  cha-mae-BUX-us - low-growing with box-like leaves
  cha-mae-DAPH-ne - a low-grow ing shrub in the Erica family
dasy - shaggy, hairy, or thick
  das-y-CLA-drus - with shaggy branches
  das-y-STE-mon - with hairy sta- mens
eri - woolly
  er-i-ANTH-er-us - woolly anthers
  er-i-a-CAN-thus - woolly spines
fili - threadlike
  fil-IF-er-a - thread-bearing
  fil-i-FOR-mis - thread-like

45

hetero - diverse
> *he-TER-o-don* - diversely toothed
> *he-ter-o-LE-pis* - diversely scaled

holo - completely
> *ho-lo-CAR-pus* - fruit not split or lobed
> *ho-lo-PE-ta-lus* - entire, undivided petals

lasi - woolly
> *las-i-AN-drus* - with woolly stamens
> *las-i-CAR-pus* - with woolly fruit

lepto - slender, thin
> *lep-TO-cla-dus* - thin branches
> *LEP-to-pus* - thin stalks

macro - big or large
> *ma-cro-PHYL-lus* - big leaves
> *mac-ro-RHI-zus* - big roots

mega - big
> *me-ga-LAN-thus* - with large flowers
> *me-ga-SPER-mus* - with big seeds

micro - small
> *mi-cro-DAS-ys* - small and shaggy
> *mi-cro-GLOS-sus* - small tongue

multi - many
> *mul-ti-CAU-lis* - many stems
> *mul-TIF-i-dus* - many times divided

myri - many
> *myr-i-o-CAR-pus* - many seeds
> *myr-i-o-PHYL-lus* - many leaves

ortho - upright, straight
> *or-THOB-o-trys* - upright clusters
> *or-THOP-ter-us* - straight wings

pachy - thick
> *pach-y-AN-thus* - with thick flowers
> *pa-CHYP-o-dus* - with thick stalks

platy - broad
> *plat-y-PE-ta-lus* - *with* thick petals
> plat-y-PHYL-lus - with thick leaves

poly - many
> *po-ly-BO-trys* -with many clusters
> *po-ly-CHRO-mus* -with many colors

seti - bristled
> *se-ti-FOL-i-us* - with bristly or bristle-like leaves
> *se-TIG-er-us* - bristly

steno - narrow
> *sten-OP-te-rus* -with narrow wings
> *ste-no-STACH-ys* - with narrow spikes

strepto - twisted
> *strep-to-CAR-pus* - with twisted fruit
> *strep-TO-pus* - twisted stalk

sub - somewhat, rather, almost or partially
> *sub-a-CAU-lis* - not much stem, somewhat stemless
> *sub-au-ric-u-LA-tus* - partially eared, somewhat eared

tricho - hairy
> *trich-o-SAN-thus* - with hairy flowers

46

Once again I have only listed the masculine form in the examples to simplify the list. The ending will change depending on the gender of the generic name.

There are two other groups of prefixes which appear regularly: those indicating colors (which we looked at in earlier columns), and those indicating numbers (***uni, mono, bi, tri, quad, quint, penta***, etc.).

I've given you a couple of examples for each of these prefixes, but in actuality they appear over and over in botanical Latin. These prefixes and the plant parts we covered before give you the keys you need to understand, decipher and pronounce many Latin names.

Taking the Next Steps

See the Resemblance

Now that you have at least a nodding acquaintance with some Latin root words and some often used prefixes, you should be a little more comfortable with the idea that botanical Latin names are descriptive. Taking that process one step further, let's now look at some plants whose names tell us that they look like another plant.

Do you remember the earlier discussion about leaf shape determining a plant's name? Plants with toothed leaves might be called *dentata* (den-TAY-ta); plants with leaves shaped like a hand might be called *palmata* (pal-MAY-ta); and plants with heart-shaped leaves might be named *cordata* (kor-DAY-ta), etc. The Latin name gives us a picture of the leaf shape.

Now picture a maple leaf. We all have a pretty good idea of what the basic maple leaf looks like. So why not use that mental picture to name a plant with a maple-like leaf *acerifolia* (ay-ser-i-FOL-ee-a)? That is, in fact a fairly common way botanists describe plants. They use the generic name of one plant to describe another that looks similar.

Some frequently used generic names include:

Aesculus (ES-kew-lus) - horse chestnut

Alnus (AL-nus) - alder

Betula (BE-tew-la) - birch

Buxus (BUX-us) - boxwood

Ilex (I-lex) - holly, which appears in specific names as *ilici-*

Prunus (PREW-nus) - cherry or plum

Quercus (KWER-kus) - oak

Salix (SAY-lix) - willow, which appears as *salici-*

Sambucus (sam-BEW-kus) - elderberry

Rodgersias, a close relative of *Astilbe*, are currently very "in" plants to have in your shady gardens and they are named according to their leaf shapes: *Rodgersia aesculifolia* (rod-JER-zee-a es-kew-li-FOL-lee-a) with leaves like horse chestnuts; *R. pinnata* (pin-NAY-ta) with pinnate leaves which are arranged sort of like a feather; *R. podophylla* (poh-doh-FIL-la) with leaves like the May-apple (*Podophyllum*); and *R. sambucifolia* (sam-bew-si-FOL-lee-a) with leaves like an elderberry. One other *Rodgersia* has been reclassified into its own genus. It is now called *Astilboides tabularis* (a-stil-BOY-deez ta-bew-LA-ris) (syn. *R. tabularis*) for its broad, peltate leaves that look like tabletops.

The name *Astilboides* illustrates another way of saying it looks like something else. Whenever you see *-oides*, or *-opsis* at the end of a name, it means that the plant looks like something else. At a garden near me there is a *Parrotia persica* (pa-ROH-tee-a PER-si-ka) tree and a *Parrotiopsis jacquemontiana* (pa-roh-ti-OP-sis jack-mon-tee-AY-na). Both are members of the witch hazel family. The leaves of the *Parrotiopsis* look like those of the *Parrotia*. Our native Western red cedar and the arbor-vitae which many of us have in our yards are members of the genus *Thuja* (THEW-ya). There is another member of the cypress family called *Thujopsis dolobrata* (thew-YOP-sis doh-loh-BRAY-ta) named for its similarity to the *Thuja* species.

So, we now have more clues to the meaning of these sometimes long Latin names, and, hopefully, we can begin to see the pictures the botanists have painted for us when they refer to plants that look like one another. In the case of the *Rodgersia*, don't expect miracles. I still have trouble distinguishing *R. pinnata*, from *R. sambucifolia* and *R. aesculifolia.* But I keep trying.

What's in a Name?

A couple of years ago I purchased a delightful begonia called 'Looking Glass.' It was a beautifully proportioned plant with leaves that shimmered with silver. Before long, however, it began to get leggy and straggly. Over the years I have taken cuttings, pinched back tips, and moved the plant from one location to another in the vain attempt to regain its compact and full form. Then on Christmas morning, while pouring over a new plant encyclopedia, I solved my problem.

I learned *Begonia* 'Looking Glass' belongs to the "cane-like" group of begonias. These typically grow two to six feet tall. No wonder my plant would not stay compact like a nice Rex begonia. Although, I now know what to expect, the experience makes me appreciate, yet again, the value of botanical names, especially those that tell us something important about a particular species.

If my plant had been identified as *Begonia elatus* (ee-LAY-tus), *B. altus* (AL-tus) or *B. excelsus* (ex-SEL-sus), all of which mean tall, I might have anticipated a leggy rather than a compact plant. Taking this idea to the extreme, one could expect a plant with the specific epithet *arboreus* (ar-BOR-ee-us) to be tree-like.

At the other end of the size spectrum we find low-growing plants with specific epithets like: ***chamae-*** (ka-mee) on the ground; ***humilis*** (HEW-mi-lis) dwarf or low-growing; or, ***nana*** (NA-na) dwarf. ***Procumbens*** (pro-KUM-benz) and ***supinus*** (soo-PYE-nus) indicate a prostrate habit while ***repens*** (RE-penz) and ***reptans*** (REP-tanz) describe a creeping one.

Perhaps even more important to the successful cultivation of a plant is knowing where and under what conditions the plant grows in the wild. Thumbing through nursery catalogs or plant encyclopedias, it's all too easy to get swept up by the delicious descriptions. Sometimes we can get helpful clues to a plant's suitability for our gardens from its name. While plants can be very adaptable, you cannot expect a plant that grows naturally along stream beds to be happy in your dry xeriscape garden. Nor can you expect a plant that comes from the edge of a glacier to be happy in your hot, south-facing garden.

Plants that naturally occur in mountainous areas or that grow among the rocks may be happiest in a rock or scree garden. The specific epithets of plants that come from hilly or mountainous areas include:

- *alpestris* (al-PES-tris) growing in low mountains,
- *alpinus* (al-PYE-nus) and *alpicola* (al-PI-koh-la) from the high mountains, and
- *collinus* (koh-LYE-nus) growing in the hills.

Good drainage would be a requisite for plants with these names.

Also preferring good drainage are plants that inhabit rocky areas. Rock-dwellers have names like:

- *rupestris* (roo-PES-tris),
- *rupicola* (roo-PI-koh-la),
- *saxatilis* (sax-A-ti-lis) and
- *saxosus* (sax-OH-sus).

For the flower show challenge class this year, entrants are growing *Lewisia columbiana* ssp. *rupicola* (lew-ISS-ee-a koh-lum-bee-AY-na roo-PI-koh-la) which grows in rocky cliffs and definitely needs excellent drainage. The Rocky Mountain juniper is *Juniperus scopulorum* (jew-NI-per-us skop-yew-LOH-rum) because it grows in the cliffs and in dry rocky soils.

I have a boggy area in my garden which no amount of soil amendment seems to help, so I have finally given in and am actively seeking plants that tolerate wet feet. When I see specific names like

- *fluviatilis* (flew-vee-A-ti-lis),
- *rivalis* (ri-VA-lis),
- *rivularis* (ri-vew-LAY-ris) and
- *riparius* (ri-PA-ree-us),

I pay attention. Each of these names indicates that the plant grows along or in a stream and wet feet will be no problem.

I have a *Trillium rivale* (TRIL-ee-um ri-VAH-lee) planted in a moist, shady place in my garden. In the Siskiyou Mountains, it grows in wet seeps very close to the wet-loving pitcher plant *Darlingtonia californica.* (dar-ling-TOH-nee-a kal-i-FOR-nee-a).

Many plants are sun-lovers that can take the heat but those with specific names like *sylvestris* (sil-VES-tris) or *sylvaticus* (sil-VA-ti-kus) probably will not tolerate full sun. These names indicate they come from the forest and probably prefer at least part shade.

Likewise plants with names such as *frigidus* (fri-ji-dus) or *glacialis* (gla-see-AY-lis) would probably prefer a cold climate or cool feet at the very least. The specific epithets *nivalis* (ni-VA-lis), *niveus* (NI-vee-us), or *nivosus* (ni-VOH-sus) are used both for plants living in the snow or those that are snow white in color.

Last fall I purchased a new *Trillium nivale* (ni-VA-lee) which is native in the upper mid-western section of the country. It is commonly called the snow trillium because it blooms so early its flowers are frequently buried in the late snows. It is so cold hardy that it will continue to bloom and set seed despite enduring sub-freezing temperatures night after night. Its preference for glacial soils also attests to its snow hardiness.

We should be aware of the assistance to be had in some botanical names. While they don't always tell us something about the plant, sometimes they can be the key to putting the right plant in the right place

It's Greek to Me

Although we call it botanical Latin, we find a lot of Greek words and elements in plant nomenclature. The practice started back in Roman times with Pliny. When he first began to translate Greek writings about plants into Latin, he replaced the Greek names with Latin ones. For example, he used **salix** (SAY-lix) for the Greek *itea* (EYE-tee-a), **quercus** (KWER-kus) for **drys**, (dries) and **ulmus** (UL-mus) for **ptelea** (TE-lee-a). Eventually, however, he ran out of available Latin names. Then he started to transliterate the Greek names into Roman characters. Botanists have used Greek names and word elements ever since. Not only did they go back and reuse the Greek replaced by Pliny with Latin, but they found Greek uniquely suited to forming descriptive compound names.

To describe a tree-like form in Latin, the plant was typically given the specific name of **arborescens**, (ar-bor-ESS-enz) or **arboreus** (ar-BOR-ee-us). The Greek word for tree is **dendron** (DEN-dron), which is easily combined with other Greek terms to form picturesque names that can be used as the generic name. *Rhododendron* (roh-doh-DEN-dron) jumps quickly to mind. It comes from the Greek *rhodon* for rose added to tree (rose tree). The Greek name was actually given to a rose-flowered oleander before being transferred to this genus but it is still an apt word picture.

Oxydendrum (ox-ee-DEN-drum) is a single member genus which uses the Greek *oxys* meaning acid to refer to the bitter foliage of this tree. Incidently, the botanists were not afraid to reinforce their descriptions by repetition. The full name of the Sourwood tree, a native of the east coast, is *Oxydendrum arboreum*. There is a *Rhododendron arboreum* and a *R. arborescens* as well. While *R. arboreum* is, in fact, tree-like growing to some 50 feet, *R. arborescens*, a native of southeastern U.S. is rarely tree-like growing only to about about 9 feet.

A quick perusal of some botanical books revealed a number of genera that include **dendron** in their name. Here are some I have seen in Portland gardens. *Clerodendrum trichotomum* (kle-roh-DEN-drum tri-koh-TOH-mum) is a small tree, that blooms in Portland about the first of September, the leaves of which smell like peanut butter when crushed. Its name comes from the Greek *kleros* meaning chance, a reference to variable medicinal properties of the 400 or so species in this genus. There is also a *Clerodendrum* which is popular in California gardens and marginally hardy here. It is *C. bungei* (BUN-jee-eye), the glory bower. The specific name honors a Russian botanist, Alexander von Bunge (1803-1890).

Another California plant that would be marginally hardy here is *Fremontodendron californicum* (free-mon-toh-DEN-dron kal-i-FOR-ni-kum), the flannel bush. The name, of course, literally means Fremont's tree and is named for John C. Fremont its discoverer. The tulip tree, *Liriodendron* (li-ree-oh-DEN-dron) gets its name from the Greek *leirion* for a lily. The tulip-shaped blooms of *L. tulipifera* (too-lip-IF-er-a), a North American native, certainly resemble that member of the lily family. There is also a *Liriodendron* native to China.

The Sequoia is another plant with a repetitious name, *Sequoiadendron giganteum* (se-quoi-a-DEN-dron jie-gan-TEE-um). *Sequoia* means big in Greek so you have a big tree described literally as a gigantic big tree. Those of you who have toured Elk Rock garden or Jane Platt's garden will have seen the *Trochodendron aralioides* (tro-koh-DEN-dron a-ray-lee-OY-deez) or wheel-stamen tree. A native of Japan, Korea and Taiwan, it gets its name from the wheel-like arrangement of the stamens in its green flowers. *Trochos* is Greek for wheel.

Dendranthema (den-DRAN-the-ma) which until recently was considered a *Chrysanthemum* (kris-SAN-the-mum), got its name from the Greek *anthema* meaning flower. Literally the tree flower, this shrubby perennial bears its flowers on woody stems.

Indoors I suspect all of you have at one time or another grown a *Philodendron* (fil-loh-DEN-dron). This rambling climber gets its name from *phileo* the Greek for love because of its love for climbing up in trees. Visitors to the tropics will have seen these "house plants" scrambling up massive trees.

While you may have grown *Dendranthema* or *Philodendron* in your garden or house, you probably have only seen the shrub *Crinodendron* (krye-noh-DEN-dron) in California or British gardens. A native of Chile, it gets its name from the Greek *krinon* for lily. To me the pendant bell-shaped flowers bear a stronger resemblance to members of the heath family than to lilies.

Another tree hardy in our hardiness Zone 8 but rarely cultivated in gardens is the *Phellodendron* (fel-loh-DEN-dron). Known as the cork tree, its name comes from the Greek *phellos*, meaning cork. There are 10 species of these Asian natives that are all hardy in Portland. They are grown for their attractive habit, deeply furrowed bark and aromatic foliage, but they do not produce commercial cork. That comes from *Quercus suber* (KWER-kus SOO-ber), the cork oak.

I found a few other genera which use *dendron* in their names. There is the cape chestnut from South Africa, *Calodendrum capense* (ka-loh-DEN-drum kay-PEN-sa). *Kalos* is Greek for beautiful. It is a member of the *Rutaceae* (roo-TAY-see-ee), the same family as citrus.

There are some 500 members of the orchid genus *Epidendrum* (epi-DEN-drum). Taking their name from the Greek *epi* for upon, these are epiphytic or tree-perching orchids. They live on the trees, but are not parasitic.

Halimodendron halodendron (ha-li-moh-DEN-dron ha-loh-DEN-dron), the salt tree, grows in central Asia. Its name derives from the Greek *halimos* meaning salt. Once again the name is sort of overkill isn't it?

Botanical nomenclature abounds with plant names taken from Greek words. I hope you had fun with our *dendron* examples. There are many plant names with Greek origins and we'll look at some of them in future columns.

Grecian Beauty

Walk with people through a garden in bloom and you'll hear the word "beautiful" used over and over again. The Greek words for beauty and beautiful, **kallos** and **kalos**, have been used by botanists over the years to form numerous plant names.

What comes first to your mind? For me it was the Calla lily, *Calla palustris* (KA-la pa-LUS-tris). Quite literally, this is a beautiful marsh dweller. A description repeated in its common name, Bog arum. Native to north and central Europe, Asia and North America, it's the only member of its genus. It's not, however, what we normally mean when we think of "calla lily." That plant is actually another arum, *Zantedeschia aethiopica* (san-te-DESH-ee-a ee-the-OH-pi-ka). No Greek influence there. There is also a tropical creeper called *Callisia* (ka-LEEZ-ee-a), a relative of *Tradescantia* (tray-des-KAN-shee-a), that is native to tropical North and South America.

Many of you are familiar with the delightful purple berries of *Callicarpa* (ka-li-KAR-pa), aptly called Beautyberry. The species that sells so well at Market Basket is *C. bodinieri* var. *giraldii* 'Profusion' (bo-di-nee-ER-ee ji-RAL-dee-eye). But there are some 140 other species that produce white, red, pink or purple berries. *Callicarpa dichotoma* (dye-KO-to-ma), from China and Japan, grows in a pleasing arching shape and produces pinkish/purple fruits. Its specific epithet comes from its habit of repeatedly dividing into two branches. There is also *C. americana* (am-er-i-KAN-a) that is native from Virginia to Texas and in the West Indies. Although the species has violet fruit, there is a white fruited variety *C. a.* var. *lactea* (LAK-tee-a). And another species loved for its purple berries is *C. japonica* (ja-PON-i-ka).

I found two genera named for their beautiful stamens. One is the Powderpuff tree of the tropics, *Calliandra* (kal-li-AN-dra), whose name literally means beautiful male from the Greek *andros*. The flowers of members of this genus resemble colorful puff balls. The male parts, or stamens, stick out well beyond the other flower parts. The Bottlebrush from Australia, *Callistemon* (ka-li-STEE-mon), is another genus named for its lovely stamens. You have probably seen this growing in California and other warm places. The blossoms really do look like old fashioned bottle brushes.

From *kome* (KOH-me), the Greek for hair, we get *Callicoma serratifolia* (ka-li-KOH-ma se-ra-ti-FOL-ee-a), another Australian native. This tree produces globular flower heads with conspicuous creamy white stamens. Do you remember what *serratifolia* means? If you said a plant having toothed leaves, you are right. The Water starwort, *Callitriche* (ka-LEE-tri-kee), also gets its name from a Greek word for hair (*trichos*). It describes the fine, feathery foliage of these aquatic plants.

Callistephus chinensis (ka-LEE-ste-fus chi-NEN-sis) is the beautiful annual China aster we love so much in our late summer gardens. It's named for the big showy flower heads from the Greek *stephos* for crown.

For you number lovers, there is a genus called *Callitris* (ka-LEE-tris), which celebrates the beautiful mathematical arrangement of its parts. Taken from the Greek *treis* (three), the botanist who named this genus of 17 coniferous trees must have loved the three-fold pattern of leaves and conescales. Or perhaps he just sought more precision than its common name Cypress pine afforded this Australian native.

The Greek language has two words for flower, *anthos* (AN-thos) and *anthemon* (AN-thee-mon). So the name of *Callianthemum* (ka-li-AN-the-mum), a member of the Ranunculus family that is native to the mountains of central Asia and southern Europe, means, quite simply, beautiful flower.

The name of our native Incense cedar is *Calocedrus decurrens* (ka-loh-SEE-drus de-KUR-renz) or beautiful cedar. *Decurrens* describes the manner in which the leaf scales are attached to the stem. There are two other members in this genus, one from Taiwan, *C. formosana* (for-moh-SAY-na), and one from China, *C, macrolepis* (ma-kroh-LE-pis) named for its large scales.

Wildflower lovers are sure to recognize Mariposa lily, Sego lily, and Cat's ears, all common names of members of the *Calochortus* (ka-loh-KOR-tus) genus. The name is derived from the Greek for grass (*chortus*) and refers to the grasslike leaves of these lily family members.

Winter travelers to the Caribbean might see the Calaba tree in flower but that was not what caught the eye of the botanist who named this one *Calophyllum calaba* (ka-loh-FIL-lum ka-LA-ba). It was instead the beautiful heavily-veined leaves of this plant that he described in the name.

There is a terrestrial orchid that grows in parts of North America called *Calopogon* (ka-loh-POH-gon). The lip of the flower has beard-like hairs. Hence the name that means beautiful beard.

There are two more Australian natives with "beautiful" in their names. One is *Calostemma* (ka-loh-STE-ma), a member of the *Amaryllidaceae* (a-ma-ri-lid-AY-see-ee). *Calostemma pupureum* (pur-PUR-ee-um) or Garland lily and *C. lutem* (LEW-tee-um) the Australian daffodil have something in common that gives them their name. Their coronas are toothed and form a sort of wreath shape. The other genus is *Calothamnus* (ka-loh-THAM-nus). The name literally means beautiful bush from **thamnos**, the Greek for shrub or bush.

How many of you are familiar with the Rabbit-brush which thrives in the sagebrush country of central and eastern Oregon and other high desert areas? Its name *Chrysothamnus* (kris-oh-THAM-nus), literally golden bush, is an apt description of its golden yellow flowers.

We covered a lot of plant names in this column, and I'm sure I won't remember all that I read about each genus. But I will remember what "calli" and "calo" mean when used in compound words. We learned our multiplication tables by memorization. We repeated them over and over until we knew them. The same principle of repetition works with botanical Latin. Give it a try. Who knows, the exercise might just improve our memories as well as our Latin.

Forms, Varieties, Clones, Cultivars....Oh My!

I frequently hear grumbles from gardeners who are confused by the terms "cultivar," "hybrid," "variety," "form," "selection," "clone," which complicate and confuse botanical Latin terminology. A quick look back at their origin will help sort them out. After Linnaeus developed the system of binomial nomenclature, giving us the generic and specific names for plants, terminology would have been simple except for two things:

1. Throughout history people have selected and cultivated plants that produced better crops, prettier flowers, tastier fruit, etc. Eventually these selections or new varieties needed to be named; and

2. Botanists discovered that plants of the same species developed differently in various locations, and these slightly different varieties needed to be described or named.

For a while both the growers and the botanists used the same system for describing varieties and forms in botanical names by adding "**var**." (for *varietas*) or "**f**." (for *forma*) after the specific name and before the other name. But confusion mounted as to whether the varieties or forms happened in the wild or were man-made. Separate systems were required: one for the botanists describing naturally-occurring forms or varieties and one for growers who were breeding or selecting for certain traits.

In 1953, to help settle the problem, W. T. Stearn published his *International Code of Nomenclature for Cultivated Plants*, in which he coined the term "cultivar," (meaning "cultivated variety") to refer to plants selected and cultivated by growers for ornamental or economic purposes, thereby reserving the terms *varietas* and *forma* for plants found in the wild. When the cultivar name is written, it is capitalized and put between single quotation marks. It is not italicized. An example is *Magnolia grandiflora* `Edith Bogue'.

Sometimes growers cross one species with another and create a hybrid species. The resulting hybrid species is indicated by an "**x**" between the generic and specific name (*Magnolia* x *soulangiana*). If further selections of this hybrid species are made over time, you get a name like *Magnolia* x *soulangiana* `Picture` or *Viburnum* x *bodnantense* `Dawn`. When cultivars are the result of many layers of hybridizing, the growers may simply add the cultivar name to the genus as in *Rhododendron* `Cynthia`.

If you aren't hopelessly confused by now, perhaps you can see that the additional names are an effort to describe the plant in ever-greater detail. For plant variations found in the wild, botanists use the terms **subspecies (ssp.)**, *varietas* **(var.)**, and *forma* **(f.)** to describe plants in greater detail. The differences between these terms are minor but important. *Hortus Third* describes **subspecies** as a major division of a species. It is often used to denote a distinct geographic distribution of the plant (*Hortus Third* p.1223).

Variety is a subdivision of a species ranking between *subspecies* and *forma*. (*Hortus Third* p. 1225). Michael Dirr notes that a *variety* exhibits a distinct, though perhaps inconspicuous, difference from the species. *Varieties* tend to breed true to the difference (Dirr p. 976).

Forma is the lowest ranking subdivision of a species and is normally used to denote minor differences such as flower color, or leaf lobing. *Forms*, according to Dirr, typically do not breed true and do not develop natural populations or distributions (Dirr p. 963).

Sometimes, presumably to save words, the descriptions are shortened and the "var.," "f.," or "ssp." is left out. Then you see names like *Cedrus atlantica glauca pendula* (the weeping, blue atlas cedar).

To see how all of this works, let's look at a listing under magnolias in *The Hillier Manual of Trees and Shrubs*. There we find:

Magnolia campbellii

f. *alba*

`Darjeeling`

`Ethel Hillier`

`Kew's Surprise`...etc.

Showing us that there is a naturally-occurring white form and a number of cultivars or "cultivated varieties" developed by selective breeding.

Wildflower books often describe naturally-occurring varieties of species. For example, Russ Jolley's *Wildflowers of the Columbia Gorge* describes two black hawthorns found in the Gorge as *Crataegus douglasii* var. *douglasii* (found in the middle section of the Gorge) and *Crataegus douglasii* var. *suksdorfii* (a closely related variety found in the west end of the Gorge). Although the differences are probably not great, or maybe even easily discernable to most of us, they are important for scientific accuracy.

If you think of botanical Latin as being a precise way of describing plants, it won't seem so daunting. Also, if you learn the rules for writing it, it will make more sense to you. Ideally, the Latin name is in italics, but even without italics, the rules remain:

1. Capitalize the genus;
2. Do not capitalize the species;
3. Enclose cultivar name in single quotation marks, capitalize the first letter but do not italicize.

For wild plants,

4. Abbreviate variety, form, or subspecies (var., f., or ssp.) Italicize but do not capitalize the Latin varietal name. For example:

> *Magnolia grandiflora* 'Edith Bogue'
> *Magnolia* x *soulangiana* 'Picture'
> *Crataegus douglasii* var. *douglasii.*

The more you use botanical Latin, the more sense it makes and the easier it becomes. With a little practice you too can sound and write like a "pro".

A Closer Look

Read the Book...But How?

Do you ever feel when you're reading the descriptions of plants in some wild-flower books or in reference books like the Mark Griffith's *Index of Garden Plants* (which is often referred to as the RHS Dictionary because it is the index to the multi-volume tome The *RHS Dictionary of Garden Plants*), that you are trying to decipher some sort of secret code? I certainly do. Perhaps, with three and a half years of Fearless Latin columns behind us, it's time to expand the scope of the column to cover more than just Latin names and meanings.

In the early columns, I tried to stick to the basics. We looked at the most commonly used Latin names and descriptive terms. The ones we see over and over again. Now we'll begin to cover a broader range of botanical terms and definitions. Where do we start? Well, I opened my *Index of Garden Plants* to a random page and found this cryptic description:

Magnolia L. Magnoliaceae. 125 evergr. or decid. shrubs or trees. Buds enveloped by silver to grey-pubesc. stipular scales. Lvs alt. or clustered, entire, petiolate. Fls stellar or cupulate, term., solitary, often fragrant; perianth seg. In whorls of 3 or more, outer whorl often sepal-like, others petaloid; sta. arranged spirally; gynoecium sessile or short-stipitate, cy-lindric to subglobose; carpels many, spirally arranged, each with 2 ovules. Fruiting cones subglobose to cylindric; seeds colorful, suspended from follicles. Jap., Himal. W. Malesia (to Java), E N Amer. To Trop. Amer.

Goodness, did you get all of that? Let's see what we can make of it. First, we know what some of this means right off the bat. We know *Magnolia* is the name of the genus and that *Magnoliaceae* indicates the magnolia family. We know the difference between evergreen and deciduous and should recognize the abbreviations for leaves (Lvs) and flowers (Fls). We should also remember from past columns that "pubescent" (pubesc.) means that something is covered with tiny soft hairs.

But what are "stipular scales?" A stipule is a bract-like appendage, usually occurring in pairs, which is attached to the base of the leafstalk or petiole. Most of you are familiar with *Magnolia x soulangiana*. In the fall, next year's buds have formed and are sealed inside a pair of fuzzy stipules. Stipules are little, paired, leaf-like appendages found at the base of the leaf stem or petiole or where leaflets attach to the petiole. They are particularly noticeable on the stem of rose leaves but are present on Magnolias as well.

The leaves (Lvs) can be alternate (alt.), as opposed to opposite, or "clustered" as they are in some species like the big-leaf magnolia (*Magnolia macrophylla*). They are entire, having smooth unnotched edges, and are "petiolate." That is, they have a leaf stalk or "petiole" attaching them to the stem as opposed to the leaves attaching directly to the stem.

The flowers (Fls) are "stellar" (starlike) or "cupulate" (cup-shaped) and are terminal (term.), occurring at the ends of the branches. They are "solitary" or single. The "perianth" is segmented (seg.). The term "perianth" refers to the whole floral envelope including both the calyx and the corolla. It's used most often when the two are not easily distinguishable. That is, when you can't tell the sepals (which are the separate parts of the calyx) from the petals, which are the separate parts of the corolla. Descriptions of magnolia flowers usually refer to the undifferentiated parts as "tepals."

In the reproductive parts of the flower, the "stamens" (sta.) are arranged spirally. The term "gynoecium" refers to the female parts of the flower or the pistil(s). These are "sessile" (having no stalk) or "short-stipiate" (having short stalks). There are many "carpels." These are the units that make up individual pistils. Each one has two "ovules." The parts of the ovary that actually develop into seed.

The cones are "subglobose" or nearly round to "cylindric" and have colorful seeds that are suspended from "follicles." A follicle is a dry fruit that splits along a single seam on one side. *Hortus Third* describes the fruit as made up of "many separate carpels congested into a `cone', seeds often red or orange, suspended at maturity by a slender thread."

In this one short description of a magnolia we have been introduced to a number of terms, many of them new to this column. Let's review them.

Petiole - the flower stalk.

Stipule - one of a pair of leaf-like appendages found at the base of the petiole in some leaves .

Perianth - the floral envelope including both the calyx and the corolla.

Calyx - collective term for the sepals.

Corolla - the inner whorl of the perianth composed of the petals.

Stamen(s) - male part of the flower, bearing the anther, usually on a filament and producing pollen.

Gynocecium - female part of the flower, synonymous with the pistil(s).

Pistil - composed of the ovary, style and stigma. A simple pistil has one carpel, a compound one may be two or more carpels.

Carpel - is a simple pistil or part of a compound pistil. It bears the ovule.

Ovule - part of ovary which actually develops into seed.

Stipitate -borne on a stalk.

Sessile - having no stem.

Follicule - dry fruit which splits along one seam.

I'm still a little confused by some of the terms which overlap. How about you? I'll have to do some more research. Just remember you can learn a lot from books like the *Index of Garden Plants* and the *A to Z Encyclopedia of Garden Plants,* jointly published by the Royal Horticultural Society and the American Horticultural Society besides what plants look like. You can learn where they originated; hence, what kind of growing conditions they might prefer; how hardy they are in your hardiness zone; and how big they will be at maturity. Books with lots of pictures, like the *A to Z Encyclopedia*, can be very helpful in identifying a plant if you only have the common name. All the information is in the books. You just need to be able to decipher it. *Index of Garden Plants* and *A to Z* have complete glossaries of terms to help you along. Take your time and do not be put off by the small print and the abbreviations.

The Shapes of Things

Over the past eight years we've covered a lot of ground and we've discussed many, dare I say hundreds of, botanical Latin terms. While I was casting about for ideas for this column, I took a look back over the columns from past years and was struck by how much I'd forgotten. So I thought it would be good to go back over some of the ground we covered earlier, but maybe take a closer, more detailed look than we did initially.

Descriptive Latin terms can be either "**absolute**" (referring to the appearance of a particular part of a plant) or "**relative**" (describing a part of a plant in relation to another part). For example, if we say a plant has "lateral spatulate" leaves, the term "lateral" is relative—expressing the relation of the leaves to the stem; while the term "spatulate" is absolute—describing the spoon-shape of the leaf.

Many absolute terms describe the shape or form of a plant or its parts, and often come straight out of your old geometry textbook. They should give you a clear picture of the plant in your mind's eye. When you see the name *conicus* (KON-i-kus) or *pryamidalis* (pyr-a-mid-DA-lis), you should see a cone shape or a pyramid. *Cylindricus* (si-LIN-dri-kus) and *tubulosus* (tube-u-LO-sus) should form the picture of a cylinder or tube. What about *spiralis* (spi-RA-lis)? Some part of the plant, or perhaps the plant itself, should be twisted into a spiral form. Easy, isn't it.

Let's try some more. *Planus* (PLAY-nus) would be flat or level. While *compressus* (kom-PRES-sus) indicates some part of the plant itself is flattened lengthwise, *depressus* (de-PRES-sus) means that a plant or a part is flattened vertically.

Juniperus communis 'Compressa,' (jew-NI-per-is kom-MEW-nis), the wonderful dwarf juniper, grows in a very tight column to two or three feet. On the other hand, *Juniperus communis* 'Depressa' is a low, essentially prostrate form of juniper that rarely exceeds four inches in height.

While *globosus* (gloh-BOH-sus) and *sphaericus* (SFEER-i-kus) indicate round globes or spheres, as in the round flower buds of *Magnolia globosa*, *ellipticus* (ee-LIP-ti-kus) indicates some part of the plant is elliptical in shape like the dangling flowers of our native *Garrya elliptica* (GAR-ree-a ee-LIP-ti-ka).

There are other familiar shapes. We talk about other peoples' pear-shaped bodies, so why not describe a plant with a pear-shaped form as *pryiformis* (py-ri-FOR-mis) using the Latin name for pear? Or call a plant with teardrop-like fruit *lachrymiformis* (lak-ri-mi-FOR-mis)? Some plants have egg-shaped parts, such as fruits or ovaries, and might be called *ovoideus* (oh-VOY-dee-us) or *ovoides* (oh-VOY-deez).

Rock gardeners are familiar with *Campanula cochleariifolia* (kam-PAN-yew-la cock-lee-a-ree-i-FOL-ee-a) and its many cultivars and with *Saxifraga cochlearis* (sax-IF-ra-ga cock-lee-AY-ris). Both of these form tight creeping tufts with leaves that are spoon-shaped from the Latin *cochlear* meaning spoon.

A plant with the name *petaloides* (pe-ta-LOY-deez) would have parts that looked like petals while one with the name *alatus* (a-LAY-tus) would have parts with wings as in *Euonymous alata* (yew-ON-i-mus a-LAY-ta), the winged euonymous that displays its brilliant red foliage each fall.

Plants with thread-like or hair-like parts might have names such as *flagelliformis* (fla-jel-i-FOR-mis) or *flagelifera* (fla-jel-IF-er-a) meaning whip-shaped, *filiformis* (fil-i-FOR-mis) or *filifera* (fil-IF-er-a) meaning thread-like, or *capillaris* (ka-pi-LA-ris) meaning hair-like.

These are but a few of the many absolute terms used to describe the general solid forms of plants or their parts. Hopefully, you'll recognize others as you come upon them when plant shopping or doing research. For a more complete list, you can take a look at William T. Stearn's *Botanical Latin,* Fourth Edition.

Outlines

Continuing with our closer look at the basics theme, this month we'll examine terms that describe planes and outlines, terms generally applied to leaf shapes. Why bother to learn these terms? Because they assist in the identification of plant species. A knowledge of the Latin terms can help you quickly solve some identification questions. If you have a plant with very round leaves, you can quickly eliminate from consideration any genera that have long narrow leaves, or triangular-shaped leaves. Often the shape of the leaf gives the plant its specific epithet. That makes things easy. But even without the name clue, plant descriptions in authoritative books use the Latin terms. (Remember that the specific epithet's ending changes with the gender of the generic name. For reasons of simplicity, I will use the masculine forms here. But you will need to recognize that *ellipticus*, *ellipitica*, and *ellipticum* are all the same word with different gender endings.)

Let's first look at terms that describe straight-sided leaves.

- *linearis* (lin-ee-A-ris) describes a short, narrow leaf with parallel sides.
- *subulatus* (sub-yew-LAY-tus) indicates an awl-shaped leaf that tapers from a relatively broad base to a narrow point,
- *acerosus* (ay-se-ROH-sus) means needle-shaped.

Another straight-sided, pointed form is sword-shaped. There are two terms for this: *ensiformis* (en-si-FOR-mis) or *gladiatus* (gla-dee-AY-tus). Both indicate a leaf that is quite straight, with parallel veins and an acute point at the apex. An iris is a good example.

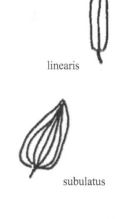

linearis

subulatus

ensiformis

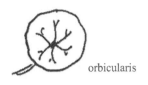

orbicularis

ellipticus

oblongus

ovatus

lanceolatus

spatulatus

deltoides

cordiformis

reniformis

Round leaves are often denoted by *orbicularis* (or-bik-yew-LA-ris) which means a perfect circle. *Rotundus* (roh-TUN-dus) would indicate a rounded leaf which may not be perfectly circular.

Three other terms for roundish leaves are often confusing. These are *ovatus*, *oblongus*, and *ellipticus*. The differences are subtle but important.

- *Ellipticus* (ee-LIP-ti-kus) indicates an oval that is acute at the ends and equally curved down the sides.

- *Ovatus* (oh-VA-tus) means an egg-shaped oval that is broadest at the lower end.

- *Oblongus* (ob-LONG-us) describes an oval that is obtuse at both ends and has parallel sides.

Basically, the differences are in the width of the curves at the top and bottom of the leaf.

A little less confusing are the terms that describe leaf outline shapes as looking like familiar things. For example:

- *Lanceolatus* (lan-see-oH-LAY-tus) describes a leaf that looks like the tip of a lance.

- *Spatulatus* (spa-tu-LAY-tus) and *spathulatus* (spath-yew-LAY-tus) use the chemist's spatula to describe a leaf shape that is ovate at the tip with a long handle-like base.

The Greek letter *delta* has a very particular triangular shape. Leaves with this shape are called deltoid. The Latin term is *deltoides* (del-TOY-deez). *Triangularis* (tri-an-gew-LA-ris) can be used for any type of three-sided shape.

Cordiformis (kor-di-FOR-mis) and *cordatus* (kor-DAY-tus) denote a shape like an inverted Valentine's Day heart. *Reniformis* (re-ni-FOR-mis) describes another organ - the kidney. This leaf forms a crescent curve with rounded ends.

A picture is probably necessary for most of us to visualize the difference between an arrowhead form and a spearhead. In Latin, *sagittatus* (sa-ji-TAY-tus) denotes the arrowhead while *hastatus* (has-TAY-tus) describes the spearhead. Note that the basal lobes of a sagittate leaf point down and outwards before the sides taper to a point at the apex. On hastate leaves, the basal lobes point straight out at nearly right angles to the stem before the sides taper to the pointed apex.

Sometimes you'll see the prefix "ob" preceding some of these names as in *obovatus, obhastatus, obcordatus*, or in descriptions as obovate, obhastate, or obcordate. This prefix tells us that the normal shape of the leaf is reversed. An obovate leaf would be broader at the top than at the base; and the stem of a obcordate leaf would attach at the pointed end and the rounded lobes would be the apex or top.

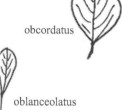

An understanding of these basic outline shapes will simplify plant identification for you. Add these to the terms we covered last month describing absolute solid forms, and you are on your way to building a firm foundation in Botanical Latin. Next month we'll look a little deeper into leaf shapes, focusing on the tip (apex) and base forms.

Apex and Base Shapes

This month we move on to terms relating to the tips and bases of leaves. One caveat. My drawing ability is almost nonexistent so feel free to check out the professional drawings in your favorite botanical text like *Hortus Third, The Index of Garden Plants* (better known as the RHS Dictionary) or my source, Stearn's *Botanical Latin* (4th Ed.).

The shape, including the hardness and sharpness of the point, at the apex or tip of the leaf is frequently the key to differentiating one plant from other members of its genus. There are several names for leaves with hard points. One is *aristatus* (a-ris-TAY-tus) meaning "awned" or one abruptly ending in a hard, straight, bristle-like point which is an extension of the midrib. *Mucronatus* (mew-kroh-NAY-tus) and its diminuative form *mucronulatus* (mew-kron-yew-LAY-tus) describe a very short hard point at the tip with no tapering of the leaf. When the leaf tapers to a short, rigid point, the Latin is *cuspidatus* (kus-pi-DAY-tus).

Some terms are fairly subjective. *Pungens* (PUN-jenz) is defined as ending gradually in a sharp point while *setosus* (se-TOH-sus) is defined as ending gradually in a very fine sharp point.

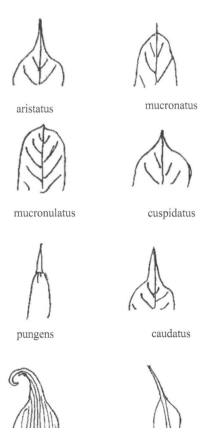

aristatus

mucronatus

mucronulatus

cuspidatus

pungens

caudatus

cirrhosus

piliferous

The important thing to remember is that *you* don't have to determine if a leaf is pungent or setose. You need only know that the leaf terminates gradually in a fine point.

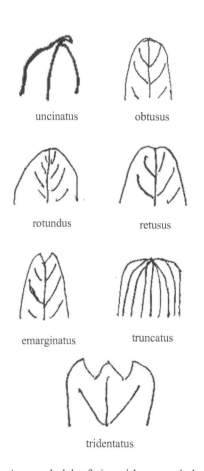

uncinatus

obtusus

rotundus

retusus

emarginatus

truncatus

tridentatus

Some leaves end in soft points. The term for a leaf that ends in a long weak tail-like point is *caudatus* (kaw-DAY-tus). For a leaf that is tipped with a spiraling or curling thread-like appendage, the term is *cirrhosus* (si-ROE-sus).

Piliferus (pi-LIF-er-us) means that the tip is very fine and hair-like. When the hairs at the tip of the leaf hook back abruptly it is called uncinate and the Latin is *uncinatus* (un-si-NAY-tus). Acuminate leaves taper gradually to a point. Acute leaves are similar but generally have a shorter taper.

As we well know, not all leaves end in points. One that is gradually rounded at the top might described by *obtusus* (ob-TOO-sus) while one which is rounded would be *rotundus* (ro-TUN-dus). *Retusus* (re-TOO-sus) describes a rounded leaf tip that has a small notch in the center.

A rounded leaf tip with a much larger notch in it becomes emarginate or *emarginatus* (ee-mar-ji-NAY-tus).

A leaf that appears to be abruptly cut off is called *truncatus* (trun-KAY-tus). Think of your Thanksgiving cactus, *Schlumbergera truncata* (schlum-BER-je-ra trun-KAY-ta) with its blunt leaf tips. If the end of a truncated leaf looks like a "w," the name would be *tridentatus* (tri-den-TAY-tus) meaning having three teeth.

The base shape of a plant can be just as important as that of the apex in identifying the plant. You'll be relieved to note that many of the terms describing the bases of leaves are not new. ***Rotundus***, ***obtusus***, ***truncatus***, ***acutus*** *and* ***acuminatus*** can all be applied to the base of a leaf as well as to the tip. Additionally, many of the terms we discussed last month concerning leaf outlines (like ***sagittatus***, ***hastatus***, ***reniformis***, ***cordatus*** or ***cordiformis)*** mean the same thing when applied to the base.

There are a couple of additional terms I would like to add. One is ***attenuatus*** (a-ten-yew-AY-tus). It refers to a base with a long point which has a fine concave taper. A leaf which is cuneate has a wedge-shaped base formed by the straight sides of the leaf converging to a point. The Latin is ***cuneatus*** (kew-nee-AY-tus). And, lastly, when the leaf has two rounded lobes that stand out from the base (sort of like sagittate point but rounded) it is called ***auriculatus*** (au-ri-ku-LAY-tus) meaning eared.

Once again I have given you a larger than normal portion of Latin terms to digest. But these terms appear so often in botanical descriptions that you will be rewarded for your efforts when you get them safely swallowed.

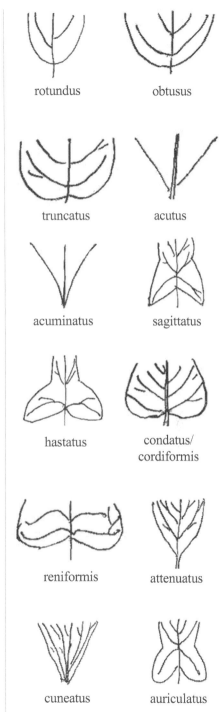

rotundus

obtusus

truncatus

acutus

acuminatus

sagittatus

hastatus

condatus/
cordiformis

reniformis

attenuatus

cuneatus

auriculatus

Leaf Margins and Divisions

This month we continue with our discussion of Latin terms for plants or plant parts that form the basis of so many botanical names. By way of a quick review, we have so far discussed:

1. General solid forms such as *globosus* (gloh-BOH-sus), *pyramidalis* (py-ra-mid-DA-lis), and *cylindricus* (si-LIN-dri-kus);

2. Outlines and plane shapes such as *ellipticus* (ee-LIP-ti-kus), *linearis* (li-nee-AY-ris), and *oblongus* (ob-LONG-us);

3. Whole leaf shapes like *sagittatus* (sa-ji-TAY-tus), *cordatus* (kor-DAY-tus, and *undulatus* (un-dew-LAY-tus); and

4. Tips and bases of leaves including tips like *aristatus* (a-ris-TAY-tus), *pungens* (PUN-jenz), *truncatus* (trun-KAY-tus), *piliferus* (pi-LI-fer-us), and *retusus* (re-TOO-sus) and bases such as *acuminatus* (a-kew-mi-NAY-tus), *hastatus* (has-TAY-tus), and *reniformis* (ren-ni-FOR-mis).

Now we turn our attention to the margins of leaves and the way they are incised to find more descriptive terms. *Note: All of the illustrations in this column are taken from Stearn's Botanical Latin, 4th Ed..*

The term that describes a leaf with a smooth or entire margin, one having no indentations or breaks, is *integer* (IN-te-jer) or *integerrimus* (in-te-JER-ri-mus).

Crenatus (kre-NAY-tus) describes a leaf with convex teeth or rounded bumps along the margin. While *dentatus* (den-TAY-tus) describes a leaf with concave teeth or those that point outward. *Denticulatus* (den-tik-yew-LAY-tus) is the diminutive form and

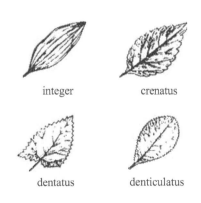

integer   crenatus

dentatus   denticulatus

Stearn (1992),p 320 (afterMarion E, Ruff in Lawrence (1955) p.70).

describes tiny concave teeth.

When the edge of the leaf is saw-like, we use the term *serratus* (ser-RAY-tus). *Serrulata* (ser-rew-LAY-tus) descibes tiny saw-like teeth. The paper-barked cherry is *Prunus serrula* (PRU-nus SER-rew-la) also has leaves with tiny saw-like margins.

The term for a leaf margin that is unevenly toothed and looks as if it might have been gnawed is *erosus* (ee-ROH-sus), and the term for a margin that is irregularly divided and twisted in curls is *cripsus* (KRIS-pus). Leaves on a plant with the name *cripsus* are generally quite crinkled or puckered.

Repandens (re-PAN-denz) de-notes another uneven margin, one that is slightly sinuous. If the uneven mar-gin is truly snake-like, combining alter-nating convex and concave curves, the term is *sinuatus* (sin-yew-AY-tus). The difference between *sinuatus* and *undulatus* is that the margin of the un-dulate leaf is wavy in two directions - it curves up and down as well as in and out, if that makes sense to you.

Some leaf margins are deeply cut or incised like many oak leaves. *Incisus* (in-SYE-sus) describes a mar-gin that is regularly and deeply cut while *lacerus* (LA-ser-us) indicates the mar-gins are deep but irregularly cut and appear to be torn into fringe-like seg-

serratus   serrulatus

Stearn (1992), p.322 (afterMarion E, Ruff in Lawrence (1955) p. 72).

erosus

crispus

repandens   sinuatus

undulatus

incisus

lacerus

Stearn (1992), p.323 (after J. Lindley (1832)).

86

ments.

Laciniatus (la-si-nee-AY-tus)
literally means slashed and denotes a
margin that is deeply divided with very
tapered and pointed incisions. Plants
with the name *laciniatus* typically have
very finely divided leaves like a lace-
leaf maple.

laciniatus

When the divisions in the leaf
margin are rounded or lobed the term is
lobatus (loh-BAY-tus). Depending on
the number of lobes the name might be
modified by the addition of a numerical
prefix such as *bilobatus* (two-lobed),
trilobatus (three-lobed), or whatever is
appropriate.

lobatus

Just as fissures are long, thin
splits in rock formations, the term *fissus*
(FISS-sus) is given to leaf margins with
long thin splits. Numerical prefixes are
often added to illustrate the number of
fissures in the leaves. For example:
bifidus (BYE-fi-dus), *trifidus* (TRI-fi-
dus), or maybe *multifidus* (mul-TI-fi-
dus).

fissus

If the splits are longer, going
nearly to the base of the leaf, the term
for the margin is *partitus* (par-TYE-tus).
As before, numerical prefixes are
often added to indicate the number of
parts.

Some leaf margins get their
names through their similarity to familiar things such as hands, fingers, feet,

partitus

Stearn (1992), p.323 (after J. Lindley (1832)).

and feathers. For example, the leaf of *Acer **palmatum*** (AY-ser pal-MAY-tum) looks like an open hand. ***Digitatus*** (di-ji-TAY-tus) would describe leaves which are finger-like and ***pedatus*** (pe-DAY-tus) leaves which resemble a bird's foot.

A feather-like leaf might be termed ***pinnatifidus*** (pi-na-TI-fi-dus) or ***pinnatipartitus*** (pi-na-ti-par-TYE-tus) depending on how deep the incising is. If the segments are very narrow and numerous making the leaf look sort of like a comb, the term is ***pectinatus*** (pek-ti-NAY-tus).

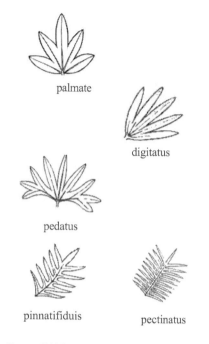

palmate

digitatus

pedatus

pinnatifiduis

pectinatus

Stearn (1992), p.323 (after J. Lindley (1832)).

Happily you don't have to make the determination as to whether a plant has feather-like, comb-like leaves, bird-foot leaves or even palm-like leaves. The names, however, should give you a mental picture and help you understand and remember plant names. All of the terms we have covered over the past four columns are terms you encounter over and over again in various forms. These are some of the basic building blocks for a good understanding of botanical Latin. You might test yourself and see how many of these plant and leaf shapes you can find in your own garden. If you know the Latin names for your plants, see how often these terms are used in those names.

On the Surface

We continue our review of the basics this month with a look at terms that describe various leaf surface features. Some of this is a bit of review as we touched on some of these terms in the "Hairy Things" chapter.

One of the first things you notice about a leaf is whether or not it is hairy. A leaf that is smooth and hairless is described as glabrous. The Latin term is *glaber* (GLA-ber). Degrees of smoothness are illustrated by **glaberrimus** (gla-BER-ri-mus) meaning totally without hairs and by **glabrescens** (gla-BRES-senz) or *glabellus* (gla-BEL-lus) indicating the presence of some hairs.

There are many terms that describe hairy leaves. I'll give you some of the most commonly used terms with their simplest definitions. For the truly curious, Mark Griffiths' *Index of Garden Plants* (*1994*) offers cross-section drawings that show the subtle differences more clearly than words. For most of us, however, just knowing a term describes a hairy surface is sufficient.

Hair Coverings

arachnoideus (a-rack-NOY-dee-us) - cobwebbed

asper (AS-per) or *scabra* (SKA-bra) - rough, covered with hard, short, rigid points.

barbatus (bar-BAY-tus) - bearded, with long weak hairs

ciliatus (sil-ee-AY-tus) - having fine hairs at the margin

farinosus (fa-ri-NOH-sus) - having a mealy covering

fimbriatus (fim-bree-AY-tus) - fringed with long thread-like appendages

hirtus (HIR-tus), or *villosus* (vi-LOH-sus) - shaggy, covered with long weak hairs

hispidus (HIS-pi-dus) - covered with long rigid hairs

lanatus (la-NAY-tus) - woolly, covered with long, curly, matted hairs

lepidotus (le-pi-DOH-tus) - covered with tiny peltate scales

papillous (pa-pi-LOH-sus) - pimpled, covered with minute bumps

peronatus (pe-ro-NAY-tus) - covered with a thick woolly substance which becomes mealy

pilosus (pi-LOH-sus) - hairy, covered with short weak hair

plumosus (plu-MOH-sus) - feathery, covered with long hairs that are themselves hairy

pubens (PEW-benz) or *pubescens (pew*-BES-senz) - downy, covered with short, weak, dense hairs

sericeus (se-RISS-ee-us) - silky, covered with very fine, close-pressed hairs

spiculatus (spi-kew-LAY-tus) - covered with fine, fleshy, erect points

spinosus (spi-NOH-sus) - spiny

squamosus (squa-MOH-sus) - scaly, covered with tiny scales fixed at one end

strigosus (strye-GOH-sus) - covered with sharp, adpressed, rigid hairs - much like *hispidus*

tomentosus (toe-men-TOE-sus) - covered with dense, rigid, short hairs

velutinus (ve-LOO-ti-nus) - velvety, much like tomentose only softer

Leaves may have a distinct surface appearance without being hairy. For example, *Rosa rugosa* (ROH-sa roo-GOH-sa) has rugose leaves that are wrinkled and covered with distinctly raised netted lines. A leaf with a clearly netted appearance but without the deep indentations of a rugose one is described by the term *reticulatus* (re-ti-kew-LAY-tus). There is no better example than the Japanese honeysuckle, *Lonicera japonica* 'Aureoreticulata' (lo-NISS-era ja-PON-i-ka au-ree-oh-re-tik-yew-LAY-ta). Its leaves are visibly netted with yellow veins. The early-blooming *Iris reticulata* gets its name from the netted or webbed covering of its bulb, not its leaves.

Striatus (strye-AY-tus) indicates a leaf surface marked with longitudinal lines. *Lineatus* (li-nee-AY-tus) means much the same thing.

Another frequently seen term describing the surface is *punctatus* (punk-TAY-tus). A punctate leaf will be covered with tiny, pin prick-like indentations. I really can't remember seeing tiny indentations in the leaves of my thuggish loosestrife, *Lysimachia punctata* (lye-si-MACH-ee-a punk-TAY-ta) before I yanked it all out. But I'll take a better look the next time I see it in someone else's garden. Below are some more terms describing texture of substance.

Substance and Texture

baccatus (bak-KAY-tus) - berried, having a juicy succulent nature

carnosus (kar-NOH-sus) - fleshy

ceraceus (se-RAY-see-us) - waxy

coriaceus (ko-ree-AY-see-us) - leathery

corneus (KOR-nee-us) - horny

corticatus (kor-ti-KAY-tus) - coated, harder on the outside than on the inside

crassus (KRAS-sus) - thick (as in *Crassula*, the jade plant)

crustaceus (krus-TAY-see-us) - hard, thin, and brittle

farinaceus (fa-ri-NAY-see-us) - mealy, having the texture of flour in a mass

fibrosus (fye-BRO-sus) - fibrous

gelatinosus (je-la-ti-NOH-sus) - jelly-like

herbaceus (her-BAY-see-us) - thin, green and cellular

laxus (LAX-us) - loose

lignosus (lig-NOH-sus) or *ligneus* (LIG-nee-us) - woody

membranaceus (mem-bran-AY-see-us) - thin, semi-transparent

scariosus (sca-ree-OH-sus) - thin, dry with shriveled appearance

succulentus (suc-kew-LEN-tus) - very cellular and juicy.

Polish or the lack thereof is yet another type of leaf texture. Below are some of the most commonly-used terms which describe this facet of leaf texture.

Polish

dealbatus (dee-al-BAY-tus) - whitened, covered with a very light white powder

glaucus (GLAU-kus) - covered with a fine "bloom" the color of a cabbage leaf - ie., it has bluish-white tinge to it.

glutinosus (glue-ti-NOH-sus) - covered with a glutinous or sticky exudation

laevigatus (lee-vi-GAY-tus) - polished

laevis (LEE-vis) or glabra (GLA-bra) - smooth, free of hairs or any unevenness

mucosus (mew-KOH-sus) - slimy

nitidus (NI-ti-dus) - shining, having a smooth, even, polished surface

nudus (NEW-dus) or denudatus (de-new-DAY-tus) - naked, the reverse of hairy or downy

opacus (oh-PAY-kus) - dull, the reverse of shiny

splendens (SPLEN-denz) - glittering, much like polished but the surface luster is broken

I can hear some of you saying, "Whoa! This is too much!" But take heart. These terms we are applying to leaf texture and surface also apply to other parts of plants. We have already seen the example of *Iris reticulata* whose bulb is reticulated or netted rather than its leaves. So once you have mastered the terms, you can and will use them again and again. If you take a few minutes to look at the illustrations in the *Index of Garden Plants*, better known as the RHS Dictionary, you'll get a better mental picture.

Relative Direction

So far in our review this year of "the basics" of Latin descriptive terms, we have confined our study to "absolute terms." That is, terms that describe the appearance of an individual plant or plant part. We've looked at general and solid forms, outlines and planes of leaves (including tips and bases), leaf margins, division and incision, and we've studied surface markings and textures. Now we turn our attention to some "relative terms" that describe how plant parts relate to other things.

"Direction" denotes the relation plant organs bear to the earth or to the stem of the plant and "insertion" describes how one part is inserted into another. We'll start with terms of direction.

Erectus (ee-REK-tus) means pointing straight up to the sky. Flowers looking up can be described as erect. On the other hand, *rectus* (REK-tus) simply means the part is not curved or wavy; that it grows in a straight line in any direction including directly out from the stem. The term *strictus* (STRIK-tus) is the same as *rectus* only more so, as in very straight.

There are a number of terms that describe parts that are hanging or bent down. *Descendens* (de-SEN-denz) means the plant part points gradually downward. It could be the leaves or flowers in relation to a branch or the branches to the upright stem. *Ascendens* (a-SEN-denz) would, of course, be just the opposite.

Pendulus (PEN-dew-lus) means hanging down because of a weakness of the branch or support. *Dependens* (de-PEN-denz) is somewhat similar and means that the branch or leaf or flower hangs down because of its weight

Cernuus (SER-new-us) indicates drooping or an inclination a little past perpendicular so the apex is pointing at the horizon. The flowers of *Trillium cernuum* (TRIL-lee-um SER-new-um)

Cernuus

droop out and down while those of *T. nutans* (NEW-tans) nod well past perpendicular. ***Nutans*** means the apex points toward the ground.

Nutans

Sometimes organs lean rather than hang. ***Reclinatus*** (re-kli-NAY-tus) means gradually falling away from perpendicular, while ***inclinatus*** (in-kli-NAY-tus) and ***declinatus*** (de-kli-NAY-tus) mean the same thing only more so.

Verticalis (ver-ti-KA-lis) and ***perpendicularis*** (per-pen-dik-yew-LA-ris) both describe something that is at right angles to something else—perhaps branches that form right angles with the upright stem or leaves or flowers which rise vertically above a horizontal stem.

Horizontalis (hor-i-zon-TAY-lis) denotes the plane of the leaf points upward and the apex to the horizon or the whole branch faces upward with the tip to the horizon. ***Obliquus*** (ob-LYE-kwus) is somewhat the same only the margin of the leaf points skyward and the apex to the horizon.

When leaves, flower petals, or other organs are rolled, they are described in terms of the direction of the roll. The term for a part that rolls inward in ***involutus*** (in-voh-LEW-tus). The term for one that rolls up is ***convolutus*** (kon-voh-LEW-tus) and for one that rolls backward ***revolutus*** (re-voh-LEW-tus). The petals of our native fawn lily, *Erythronium revolutum* (ehr-i-THROH-nee-um re-voh-LEW-tum) curl back away from the center of the flower.

Revolute petals

Involute cross-section

revolute cross-section

Organs can also be bent away from the axis formed by the stem. To indicate various types of bends there are numerous terms based on the root words ***-flexus*** and ***-curvus***. Sudden inward bends are described by several

Curvus

94

terms including: *inflexus* (in-FLEX-us), *curvus* (KUR-vus), *introflexus* (in-troh-FLEX-us), and *introcurvus* (in-troh-KUR-vus).

Recurvus

Parts suddenly bent backwards or reflexed are described by *reflexus* (re-FLEX-us) or *recurvus* (re-KUR-vus). Similarly, parts bent downward are called *deflexus* (de-FLEX-us) or *declinatus* (de-kli-NAY-tus). *Flexuosus* (flex-yew-OH-sus) indicates a gentle bending in an alternate pattern inward and outward.

Reflexus

Deflexus

Three particular types of bends are described as: *tortuosus* (tor-tew-OH-sus)-with irregular bending and turning; *geniculatus* (je-nik-yew-LAY-tus)-jointed like a knee; and *circinatus* (sir-sin-AY-tus)-bent like a crosier or shepherd's crook.

There are several terms that describe organs that spread away from the main axis. For example, *procumbens* (proh-KUM-benz) and *humifusus* (hew-mi-FEW-sus) both describe organs that spread over the surface of the ground. *Prostratus* (pro-STRAY-tus) means much the same thing but indicates the organ is lying flat on the ground. *Diffusus* (dif-FEW-sus) simply means spreading widely. *Patens* (PAY-tens) is used to describe organs such as petals that spread gradually outward from the center, while *divaricatus* (di-var-i-KAY-tus) describes a straggling nature, but one in which the parts turn off at nearly right angles. *Decumbens* (de-KUM-benz) means the organ reclines on the ground but rises upward at the apex.

To wrap up our on-going discussion of the terms describing individual plants or plant parts, let's turn briefly to the relative terms of insertion or how things are attached. Having all ready thrown a lot of terms at you, I promise to mention only those that are commonly seen on plants at your local nursery.

Peltatus (pel-TAY-tus) and *umbilicatus* (um-bi-li-KAY-tus) both mean that the part is attached to the stalk by its center or some part distinctly inside the margin. If you are familiar with

Peltatus

the common Mayapple, *Podophyllum peltatum* (poh-doh-FIL-lum pel-TAY-tum), you know the leaf looks much like an umbrella with the stem as the handle.

Sessile (SES-ile) means without any visible stalk or sitting on the body that supports it. The blossom of *Trillium sessile* sits right on top of its whorl of leaves. *Decurrens* (dee-KUR-renz) indicates the leaf runs down the stem below the insertion point.

Some leaves clasp onto the stem. *Amplectens* (am-PLEK-tenz) means they clasp at the base, while *amplexicaulis* (am-plex-i-KAW-liss) says they clasp onto the stem. You'll remember from past columns that *caulis* in Latin compound words means stem. If the amplexicaul leaf has two basal lobes that unite around the stem, the term is *perfoliatus* (per-foh-lee-AY-tus). In this case the stem appears to pass through the body of the leaf.

Once again I've given you a bunch of terms to assimilate. Some of them are more obvious than others. You can guess that *pendulus* means something hangs down, but now you can add *cernuus* and *nutans* to that drooping picture. Additionally, the differences between some of these terms are grist for only a true botanist's mill. There will be no quiz on whether something is decumbent, or prostrate or procumbent. But some of you may find these small differences and nuances of interest. At least now you have some concept of relative terms for individual plants and plant parts.

Sessile leaf

Trillium sessile

Amplexicaulus

Perfoliate leaves

Uvularia perfoliata

Collective Terms

The descriptive Latin terms we've been studying in the last six columns have all been individual in nature. They are applied to a single plant or part of a plant, and are either absolute (*e.g.* a leaf that is cordate or heart-shaped) or relative (*e.g.* a stem that is pendulous). There are also collective terms in botanical Latin that can only be applied to plant parts in masses as in how the flowers, leaves, or other parts are arranged.

I'll bet you are already using some of these terms to identify plants. One of the first things you look for is the arrangement of the leaves, whether they are opposite (*oppositus)* [op-POS-i-tus] or alternate (*alternus*) [al-TER-nus]. Opposite leaves are directly across the stem from each other, while alternate leaves are arranged above and below each other on either side of the stem. Although we think about leaf arrangement first, these terms can also apply to other parts of a plant. For example, opposite petals would be arranged on either side of the ovary.

We are all familiar with the star magnolia, *M. stellata*, whose name describes the pattern of the numerous petals arranged star-like in opposition around a central axis. The terms *stelliformis* (stel-li-FOR-mis) and *stellulatus* (stel-yew-LAY-tus) mean the same thing.

Another term with a similar meaning is *verticillatus* (ver-ti-si-LAY-tus), literally whorled. It can apply to leaves whorled around the stem as in the Japanese umbrella pine, *Sciadopitys verticillata* (sye-a-DOP-it-iss), or to sepals, petals and stamens around the ovary.

Anyone who has researched clematis will be familiar with the term ternate (*ternus)* referring to parts in threes. In this case it is three leaves, that are positioned around the stem. Many clematis actually have triternate leaves with three groups of three leaves around the stem.

Sparsus (SPAR-sus), meaning scattered, relates to a random sort of arrangement. Applied to leaves it would indicate a lack of a formal arrangement like we see in opposite, alternate, stellate or ternate. The name for a compound arrangement of leaves or flowers is ***compositus*** (kom-POS-i-tus). This is used when several parts are united into a single whole. Umbels or racemose inflorescences are examples as are pinnate leaves. When parts such as petals or sepals are crowded and pressed closely together the term used is ***confertus*** (kon-FER-tus). If the crowded parts actually lie over one another in a regular fashion like cedar shakes on a roof, we say it is imbricated (***imbricatus***) (im-bri-KAY-tus). Picture the bud of a bachelor button.

Sometimes the crowded parts are not actually opposite one another, but seem to be because they are so closely packed around the stem like the petals of a double peony or rose. We call this arrangement rosulate. The Latin name would be ***rosulatus*** (rose-yew-LAY-tus) or ***rosularis*** (rose-yew-LA-ris). For a plant with petals or leaves arranged like those of a single rose blossom, we use the term ***rosaceus*** (rose-AY-see-us). Whether the parts are double or single, we can all visualize a rose shape and understand what the name implies.

Another term we should have little trouble with is ***radiatus*** (ray-dee-AY-tus). This describes an arrangement of petals that radiate from a common center like those of a daisy.

If the parts of a plant, such as the individual flowers in a panicle, are distant from each other and display an openness, the term ***laxus*** (LAX-us) is used. Think of the inflorescence of Queen Anne's lace or baby's breath. The little flowers that make up the head of Queen Anne's lace are tightly packed together while the tiny flowers in baby's breath are spaced much farther apart and have an airy quality about them.

Most of us are familiar with the little pink thrift, *Armeria caespitosa* (ar-MER-ee-a ses-pi-TOH-sa). Its name derives from its dense, tightly packed clump of leaves. Another type of tightly packed leaf arrangement is fasciculate. (***fasciculatus)*** [fas-sik-yew-LAY-tus]. In this arrangement the several parts spring from a common point in a bundle. The needles of the larch tree are an example.

Another term derived from the same root is ***fasciatus*** (fas-see-AY-tus). This means that several parts are growing unnaturally together into a single part. Every now and then I find a foxglove on which the last several buds at the top of the stalk have grown together into an eerie looking mass. Eventually it opens into a single distorted flower. I have also seen flower arrangers go wild for a pussy willow with mutated stems with a flat club-like appearance. This type of mutation is called fasciation.

Sometimes parts are arranged in rows and the plants are described according to the position of the rows. If the leaves are arranged in two opposite rows, the names could be *distichus* (DISS-tik-us) or *bifarius* (bye-FA-ree-us). Many conifers have distichous needles. The bald cypress, *Taxodium distichum* (tax-OH-dee-um DISS-tik-um) is named for this needle pattern.

When the parts are lined up on only one side of the stem or axis, or are turned toward one side, the terms *unilateralis* (yew-ni-la-te-RAY-liss) and *secundus* (se-KUN-dus) are used. The leaf pattern common to members of the *Labiatae* (la-bee-A-tee) or mint family, where sets of opposite leaves are alternately crossed is called *decussatus* (dee-kuss-AY-tus).

Another collective term, that we should be familiar with, is *fastigiatus* (fas-ti-jee-AY-tus). It describes an arrangement in which the parts are mostly parallel and point straight up. The Irish yew, with its rigid upright form, is *Taxus baccata* 'Fastigiata' (TAX-us ba-KAY-ta fas-ti-jee-AY-ta). If all the parts are arranged at right angles to a central axis, we describe the pattern as squarrose (*squarrosus)* [skwar-ROH-sus].

I have purposefully used both the English adjective and Latin forms for these terms. As I have mentioned before, the specific names for plants are descriptive adjectives. Learning the Latin names for plants and using them is only half of the reward you get from studying botanical Latin. The other benefit is that you can equip yourself with the descriptive terminology used by plantspeople around the world.

A Closer Look:
Summary and Quiz

Looking back through the columns of this past year, you can see we have covered a lot of terms, some familiar, some brand new, some we see frequently, and a few we find only occasionally. I know I would be hard pressed to give a specific definition for every term that has appeared in this year's columns, and I suspect most of you are somewhat shaky as well. So we'll end the year with a short review and, just for fun, another little quiz.

We spent most of the year looking at terms that apply to individual plants or plant parts. We learned that these terms are either *absolute* or *relative. Absolute* terms describe a particular shape, size or texture. *Relative* terms describe the relationship of one plant part to another:

- the position of the leaves in relation to the stem,
- the stem in relation to the horizon, or
- the flowers in relation to the branch or stem.

We discussed the shape of the whole plant in geometric terms likening them to spheres, globes, pyramids, and ovals. We also learned to describe plant parts as being shaped like a heart, a kidney, a spearhead, a lance or a feather. And we studied both the apex and base shapes of leaves. Additionally, we looked at the absolute terms for the texture, substance and polish of plant parts.

When we turned to the relative terms, we looked at how plants or their parts grow in relation to vertical and horizontal planes. Whether they were erect, leaning or prostrate; whether the leaves or flowers nodded, drooped or looked skyward; or whether parts arched or bent away from the central axis.

Finally, we looked at *collective* terms that can be applied only to plant parts in multiples. The leaves are opposite or alternate; the petals, leaves or branches are arranged in particular patterns or groupings.

Throughout the year I tried to pick terms frequently used or needed either to describe a plant or to understand its Latin name. I hope it's helped you appreciate just how useful the terminology can be.

I saw shrubs in bloom on a recent trip that I couldn't immediately identify. I took a picture of it for future reference, but I also made some mental notes in case I found someone I could ask about the plant later. I noted that the leaves were opposite, glabrous, slightly rugose, ovate to elliptical and that the fading blooms were greenish-yellow and had four small but distinctive bracts.

I have finally decided that the plants were a shrubby form, rather than tree form, of *Cornus mas*, the Japanese cornelian cherry. The plants I saw had lost most of their anthers and therefore didn't have their typical puff-ball shape. But I was able to identify the plant when I got home because I had made note of some of its key characteristics that I could then compare with those in reference books.

The beauty of botanical terminology is that descriptive definitions can and often are used as plant names. Suppose you know a genus has two species in it. One is ***oppositifolia*** (op-pos-it-i-FOL-ee-a) and the other ***alternifolia*** (al-ter-ni-FOL-ee-a). By looking at the leaf placement on the stem you can accurately identify each species. While not all identifying choices are as obvious as this example, you'll find plenty of clues to plant identification in their names. It just takes time to familiarize yourself with the necessary terms. Take little quiz on the next page just for fun and see how much you have already learned. Note: only masculine form is shown.

102

Fearless Latin Quiz

1. ____ *Asper*	A.	Plant part flattened lengthwise
2. ____ *Auriculatus*	B.	Having a ball shape
3. ____ *Compressus*	C.	Having a round outline
4. ____ *Cordatus*	D.	Having an egg shape
5. ____ *Crenatus*	E.	Lance-like
6. ____ *Denticulatus*	F.	Arrow-headed
7. ____ *Glabra*	G.	Terminating in hard sharp point
8. ____ *Glaucus*	H.	Terminating in a hair-like point
9. ____ *Globosus*	I.	Having an oblong apex
10. ____ *Hispidus*	J.	Having a rounded apex with a depression in the center
11. ____ *Integer*	K.	Having an abruptly flattened apex
12. ____ *Lanatus*	L.	Heart-shaped
13. ____ *Lanceolatus*	M.	Ear-like
14. ____ *Nitidus*	N.	Whole or entire
15. ____ *Obtusus*	O.	Having a saw-like edge
16. ____ *Ovatus*	P.	Having a toothed edge
17. ____ *Palmatus*	Q.	Having rounded bumps along edge
18. ____ *Piliferus*	R.	Feather-like
19. ____ *Pinnatus*	S.	Hand-shaped
20. ____ *Pungens*	T.	Having a rough texture or surface
21. ____ *Retusus*	U.	Covered with long rigid hairs
22. ____ *Rotundus*	V.	Woolly
23. ____ *Sagittatus*	W.	Covered with fine bloom the color of a cabbage leaf
24. ____ *Serratus*	X.	Having a polished surface
25. ____ *Truncatus*	Y.	Having a smooth surface

Answers 1T; 2M; 3A; 4L; 5Q; 6P; 7Y; 8W; 9B; 10U; 11N; 12V; 13E; 14X; 15I; 16D; 17S; 18H; 19R; 20G; 21J; 22C; 23F; 24O; 25K.

Just for Fun!

Before we continue our study of botanical Latin and how we can use it to enhance our knowledge and appreciation of plants, I thought you might enjoy this article that appeared in the April 2004 issue of The Gardeners, *and written in the spirit of April Fools' Day. My inspiration was the wonderful and fanciful botanical drawings of Edward Lear, the 19th Century artist and author who published his silliness in* The Nonsense Books. *My copy was published by Little, Brown and Company in 1917. Lear's plant drawings, absurd as they are, clearly demonstrate how plants get their botanical names. The plants are all Lear's and the text is mine.*

Not long ago a self-proclaimed faithful reader of *Fearless Latin* told me she loved the column but was still intimidated by botanical Latin (not exactly music to my ears), and by the way, how did I remember all those names? To be honest, I don't remember all the names we have covered in the 10-plus years of the column. But I know and use more botanical names than I did when I started this column. When we learned to read as children, we started with a few words; mastered them and learned some more. We continue this process all our lives, particularly if we work crossword puzzles and buy plants. The same building-block system works for botanical Latin. But it works only if you use the botanical names on a regular basis. My suggestion has always been to learn the botanical names of the plants in your garden, those that you see day in and day out, year in and year out. Then learn the botanical names of any plants you purchase for your garden and think of them as the "real names."

I learned my first botanical names as a very young child, I am told, following my dad around the garden and observing the plants I found there.

In the spring I could hardly wait for the Narcissus relative *Baccopipia gracilis* (bak-oh-PYE-pee-a GRAS-si-lis) to open. This member of the *Amaryllidaceae* or Amaryllis family is native to the southeastern U.S. Native Americans grew it close to their tobacco plants, *Nicotiana tabecum* (ni-koh-tee-AY-na tab-A-kum). Zones 5-9.

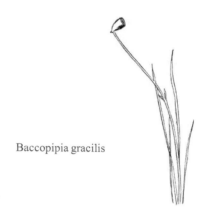

Baccopipia gracilis

Bottlephorkia spoonifolia (bot-el-FOR-kee-a spoo-ni-FOL-ee-a) belongs to the *Asteraceae* and is closely related to *Catananche* (ka-ta-NAN-kee) or Cupid's dart. The bottle-shaped center of the flower is a wonderful purple-blue color surrounded by white to pink petals. Surprisingly, this native of Peru has adapted well to urban areas where it is often found thriving behind hotels and restaurants. Zones 4-8

Bottlephorkia spoonifolia

My father was ahead of his time in growing grasses like the Mediterranean beach grass *Crabbia horrida* (KRA-bee-a HORR-id-a). If you are careful of the coral-colored tips of its inflorescence, it makes a wonderful garden plant. The aqua-blue foliage is a nice foil for many flowering perennials. Zones 8-10.

Crabbia horrida

We also had a wonderful summer-blooming relative of *Dicentra spectabilis* (dye-SEN-tra spec-TA-bi-lis) or Bleeding heart. *Manypeeplia upsidownia* (ma-nee-PEEP-lee-a up-sye-DOW-nee-a) was brought back from China in the late 1800's. The most charming feature of this perennial was the variety of colors of its blossoms. You never knew just what colorful mix you would get on each blossom stalk. Although found in woodland settings in China, this is a remarkably adaptable plant. It can take sun or shade and wet or dry soil. Zones 1-10.

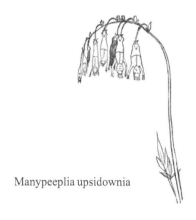

Manypeeplia upsidownia

Possibly an offshoot of the Pouch flower genus, *Calceolaria sp.* (kal-see-oh-LAR-ee-a), is *Phattfacia stupenda* (fat-FACE-ee-a stew-PEN-da). Rising about twelve inches above a rosette of basal leaves is the single large sac-like flower head that gives this genus its name. Although colors vary considerably, they generally tend to subtle shades of pink, yellow, beige and orange. When its large seed head ripens, it pops at the merest touch and spews hundreds of seeds in all directions. Most gardeners deadhead their plants before the seeds ripen. This is a plant that enjoys full sun and commands your attention. Zones 7-10.

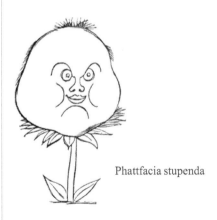

Phattfacia stupenda

We also had an orchid native to the mid-western states called

Piggwiggia pryamidalis (pig-WIG-gee-a pihr-a-mi-DAY-lis). Much like its cousin, *Spiranthes romanzoffiana* (spir-AN-theez roh-man-zoff-ee-AY-na) or Hooded ladies tresses, *Piggwiggia pyramidalis* prefers wet meadows and muddy feet. Its pinkish-white blooms open in midsummer and last several weeks. Zones 3-7.

Piggwiggia pyramidalis

A relatively rare member of the *Campanulaceae* or Bellflower family, is *Stunnia dinnerbellia* (STUN-nee-a din-ner-BEL-lee-a). At first glance it bears a resemblance to *Campanula punctata* (kam-PAN-yew-la punk-TAY-ta) with its nodding bell-shaped flowers. It is the extension of the stigma below the lip of the flower that sets *Stunnia* apart from the *Campanula*. A

Stunnia dinnerbellia

native of Siberia, *Stunnia* is an extremely hardy and dependable garden perennial. Flower colors range from pink to blue to purple. Mother always had this by the kitchen door. Zones 2-7.

A perennial favorite of mine as a child was the Tiger lily, *Tigerlillia terribilis* (tye-ger-LI-lee-a ter-ri-BI-lis). This hardy bulb from northern India was dependable even after the coldest winters. It was notable in that it had soft black and orange hairs on the backs of its petals. Unfortunately in recent years it has been replaced in most gardens by the Asian native *Lilum lancifolium* (LIL-ee-um lan-si-FOL-ee-um), syn. *L. tigrinum* (ti-GRINE-um) which is a shame to my way of thinking. Zones 4-8.

Tigerlillia terribilis

Botanical names need not be onerous. Try to find the rhythm of the names and look for the feature that gave the plant its name. Let yourself be a kid again and you will be using proper botanical names in no time.

Plant Families

Overview of Plant Families

I divide my gardening life into two periods - "BJP" (before Jane Platt) and "AJP" (after Jane Platt). In my BJP period I loved flowers, had a garden featuring perennials, and identified wild flowers by starting at the beginning of the book and turning pages until I found a flower that matched the one in front of me. What changed? Well, first, Jane Platt, an internationally known Portland plantswomen, introduced me to more ornamental plants, primarily "woodies," than I had ever seen before. She opened the door into the greater plant world which remains open today.

Once through that door I found literally thousands of plants that fascinated and challenged me. So many plants to get to know! But how to keep them all straight in my head? Botanical Latin provided the answer. Beyond giving us the generic and specific names of plants it also imposes a certain order on all the chaos. It's one thing to learn the name of a particular plant in a particular place in a particular garden. You can do that by rote. But to recognize that plant in a different setting at a different time of year or at a different stage of its life cycle is a little more difficult. So, if you don't have the time or patience to start at the beginning of your plant picture book and thumb through it until you find a matching picture every time you want to identify a plant, then you need a system you can use to eliminate the thousands of plants your specimen is not. Botanical Latin can help.

One facet of botanical Latin that I have avoided heretofore, because it is complicated by the inability of the experts to agree on a single set of definitions, is the grouping of plant *genera* into families. If you think back to your high school biology class days, you'll remember that all living things are divided into taxonomic ranks (Division, Subdivision, Class, Order, Family, Genus, Section and Species). Scientists group plants and animals on the basis of shared characteristics starting with the very broad and narrowing to the ever more specific. Memorizing the generic and specific names of plants is good, but knowing the family as well is better. When confronted with a plant that is new to you, identification is easier if you can first decide in which *Family* the plant belongs. Or, conversely if you can eliminate families to which your plant obviously does not belong. To do this you compare the basic characteristics of your plant to those of the various plant families.

Before we delve into the characteristics that are used to divide plants into families, however, I must note that there are "clumpers" and "splitters" among the botanists of the world. The clumpers combine plants into large families according to the more traditional approach. The splitters, however, have redefined many of the large families, breaking them down into smaller and more specific ones. So as not to confuse all of us hopelessly, I plan in this column to stick with the traditional clumpers and to use the RHS Dictionary (or Griffith's *Index of Garden Plants*) as the source for family definitions because I think the broader families are perhaps more familiar and easier to deal with for amateurs like ourselves.

Plants in a given family share a unique set of characteristics, primarily found in the flowers and fruits. This combination of common features sets one family apart from other families. For example, the 100 or so genera of the *Rosaceae* (rose-AY-see-ee) typically have regular flowers whose parts come in fives (petals 5, sepals 5, stamens 5). They usually have alternate leaves and a fruit that is an achene, berry, pome or drupe.

Another large family, the *Ericaceae* (air-i-KAY-see-ee) or Heath family, has about 70 genera. The members of this family prefer acid soils, and typically have simple, alternate leaves, although they can be opposite or whorled. Their flowers can be solitary or in groups, are usually regular, have a calyx that is 4-7 lobed, and a corolla that is 4-7 lobed. Their fruit is usually a capsule or berry.

Reading the definitions of typical family traits can be dizzying. But the good news is you don't have to be a botanist with a hand-lens at the ready to begin to *see* the similarities between family members.

Let's go back to the *Rosaceae* and look for similarities among its many members. First, picture a simple, wild rose like *Rosa gymnocarpa* (R. jim-noh-KAR-pa) that we find in the Columbia Gorge. Its flower is pink, single, and has five petals and many stamens clustered around the edge of the calyx. Now holding that picture in your mind, add a picture of a thimbleberry flower, *Rubus parviflorus* (ROO-bus par-vi-FLO-rus) or the Himalayan blackberry, *R. procerus* (R. pro-SEE-rus). The flowers are white, but they have the five petals with many stamens clustered around the calyx. They do look like little roses don't they? What about an apple blossom, *Malus sp.* (MAH- lus)? It has five petals and the stamens surrounding the calyx.

Here are a few more of the many genera in this family with which you are all familiar. Picture their blossoms: *Potentilla* (poh-ten-TIL-la) the cinque-foils, *Prunus* (PRU-nus) cherries, apricots and plums, *Pyrachantha* (pye-ra-KAN-tha) firethorns, *Cotoneaster* (koh-toh-nee-ASS-ter), and *Chaenomeles* (key-NOM-e-leez) flowering quince. Can you see the similarities in their blossoms? If you think small and look carefully at *Spiraea* sp. (spy-REE-a), *Holodiscus discolor* (hoh-loh-DIS-kus DIS-kol-or (Ocean spray), and mountain ash, *Sorbus* sp. (SOR-bus), you'll see tiny five-petalled flowers.

Fruits also show comparable features. Picture a rose hip in your mind. Looks pretty much like a small misshapen apple or like a small pear doesn't it. Compare those to a fruit of a hawthorn or a mountain ash. Don't they look like tiny apples? Now consider a raspberry, a thimbleberry, a salmon berry, and a strawberry. Can you see the similarities?

In groups within this large family there are similarities in the leaves as well. The leaves of a rose look very much like the leaves of *Sorbus, Acaena (*A-SEE-na*)* New Zealand burr, *Potentilla, Fragaria* (fra-GAY-ree-a) strawberry, *Geum* (JEE-um) avens, and *Sorbaria* (sor-BAY-ree-a) false spiraea. Members of another group including *Stephanandra* (ste-fan-AN-dra), *Neillia*, (NEIL-ee-a) and *Physocarpus* (fye-zoh-KAR-pus) ninebark, have leaves reminiscent of many Spiraeas.

Members of the Lily family, the *Liliaceae* (li-lee-AY-see-ee) are all mono-cotyledons. Their first leaf from seed is a single grass-like blade. They all grow from bulbs, corms or rhizomes and their showy flowers typically have parts in cycles of three. For fruit, they typically make either a berry as you see on many lilies or a capusule like those of *Camassia* (ka-MASS-ee-a).

There will be no test on the information above. These examples serve only to show that knowing what family a plant belongs in can be helpful. When you learn the Latin name for a plant, take the time to find out what family it's in. If you can associate your plant's characteristics with those of its family, you'll have a much better chance of identifying its relatives. You can use your mental snapshot of a plant you know to help you.

The botanists have given us some clues too. Families are named for prototypical plants: *Rosaceae, Liliaceae, Campanulaceae, Asteraceae*, etc. Although you are probably never going to learn all the families (no one has that much time on their hands!), learning the family to which your new plant belongs when you learn the Latin name will always be helpful to you.

Current research by botanists using DNA testing to classify and reclassify plants is stirring the waters of botanical nomenclature into a frenzy. When the commotion settles down, I expect we will all have to relearn a great deal about familiar plants. But that should not dissuade us from thinking in terms of family similarities to help us identify and remember the botanical names for plants.

The columns in the following pages discuss a number, but certainly not all, of the plant families. They focus on the families of some of the most common and well-loved plants with which many of us are already familiar. I hope that these columns will not only provide useful information about plants you have, or might like to have in your garden, but also reinforce your understanding and appreciation of botanical Latin as a valuable gardening "tool."

Poaceae (Graminae): Grass Family Part I

It has become apparent since I originally wrote this column that some ornamental grasses have become unwanted invasives in various parts of the country. In my Pacific Northwest garden the problem is nonexistent. However, if you live in an area where grasses have become harmful pests, please stick with learning the Latin and do not plant any invasive grasses.

As I begin the fifth year of this column I guess it's okay to confess to you that, among other things, I have a passion for ornamental grasses that truly come into their own in the garden in Autumn. I'm obviously not the only one with a great love for grasses because the trade has seen the introduction of more and more of them over the past five years or six years. Let's look at some and see what their Latin names tell us about them. The family to which grasses belong has long been called the *Gramineae* (gra-MIN-ee-eye) which literally means resembling grass. In the recent renaming of those few families that had not historically used the name of a representative genus, the family name was changed to *Poaceae* (poh-AY-see-ee) for the prototypical grass genus *Poa*, but you still see the old name in use.

A nice early-blooming grass is *Calamagrostis* (ka-la-ma-GROHS-tis). *Kalamos* is Greek for reed and *agrostis* is a particular kind of grass. From the two you get the common name Reed grass. The species you see most often is *C. acutiflora* 'Stricta' (a-kew-ti-FLO-ra). Can you figure out what the Latin means? We've seen it before. *Acuti* means sharply pointed, and *flora* means flower; while *stricta* tells us that it grows upright. Commonly called Feather Reed grass, the leaves of this clumping grass are three to four feet tall. The feathery blooms that come in early summer rise some three feet over the leaves. Sometimes you'll find *C. arundinacea* 'Karl Foerster' (a-run-din-AY-see-a) at the nursery. The two grasses are nearly identical, and I expect often confused by the nurserymen. The specific name refers to its resemblance to *Arundinaria* a grassy cane that grows in the southern U.S.

One name you should have little trouble deciphering is *Erianthus* (Air-ee-AN- thus). *Eri* is a prefix used to indicate hairy things and *anthus* is the flower. The common name dresses it up a little to Plume grass. The species we see most often is *E. ravennae* (ra-VEN-nee), the Ravenna grass of southern Europe. As part of the ongoing reclassification of some plants mentioned in the last column, this species has been reclassified as *Saccharum ravennae* (SAK-ka-rum). As you might guess, this is the genus of sugarcane and its name comes from the Greek name for the juice of the sugarcane, *sakcharon*. This is another tall clumper with leaves up to five feet and bloom stalks up to eight feet. It makes an outstanding accent plant in your garden.

One group of ornamental grasses that are not particularly new in the market (I remember my mother trying these in her garden in the late 1950's) are the fescues. The generic name *Festuca* (Fes-TOO- ka) is the Latin word for a grass stalk. Many of the specific names in this genus are color-related. A common one is *F. amethystina* (am-e-THYS-tye-na) which is also called *F. ovina* 'Glauca' in some references. I leave *amethystina* to your imagination. The *ovina* (oh-VYE-na) has to do with sheep. It most likely was the native grass where the sheep were pastured. *Glauca* (GLAU-kus) as you may remember means the plant has a whitish powdery finish on it. Another fescue is *F. cinerea* (si-NE-ree-a) whose name describes its grayish color.

A pair of dwarf fescues I'd love to have in my rock garden are *F. scoparia* and *F. tenuifolia* (ten-yew-i-FOL-ee-a) which is sometimes known as *F. capillata* (ka-pil-LAY-ta). I have included them because they have names we see fairly often. *Scoparius* (skoh-PAR-ee-us) means broom-like. Wildflower walkers will be familiar with the low-growing Grouseberry, *Vaccinium scoparium* (vak-SIN-ee-um skoh-PAR-ee-um). *Tenuifolia* indicates very thin hairlike leaves and *capillata* fine tiny hairs. Both are descriptive of this tiny fescue.

Some of the showiest grasses belong to the genus *Miscanthus* (mis-KAN-thus) whose name is descriptive of the stalked spiklets of the flowers from the Greek *miskos* (stem) and *anthos* (flower). Commonly called Maiden or Silver grass, the various cultivars of the species *M. sinensis* (si-NEN-sis), meaning from

China, are a must for the mixed border. They range from the very tall (eight to ten feet) to the more modest (three to five feet). My favorite is *M. s.* 'Morning Light.' Growing in a perfect fountain shape to about five feet, its fine leaves are white striped along the margins giving it a silvery cast. When the flowers emerge in the fall, they start out maroon and eventually turn to tan. It is a variegated form of *M. s.* 'Gracillimus,' (gra-SIL-li-mus) which literally means the most graceful and slender. An apt description for the thin leaves of this grass.

Other cultivars of this species include: (1) 'Purpurescens' (pur-pur-ESS-senz) which grows to four feet with purplish-brown foliage in the fall; (2) 'Zebrinus' (ze-BRYE-nus) which has wider leaves with horizontal yellow stripes that make it look like a Zebra; (3) 'Strictus' (STRIK-tus) whose leaves look much like 'Zebrinus' but they stand rigidly upright rather than arching; (4) 'Variegatus' (va-ree-GAY-tus) whose arching leaves are beautifully striped with white; and (5) 'Yaku Jima' which is very finely textured and grows only to a modest three or four feet.

If you're looking for a truly small but elegant grass, you need look no further than *Molinia caerulea* (moh-LEE-nee-a se-REW-lee-a). *Caerulea*, as you might recall from an earlier column, indicates a pure blue color. This is not a blue grass like the blue fescues so the name most likely describes the bluish tint to the emerging flower stalks. This neat and tidy clumper grows to only about one and a half feet. The cultivar 'Variegata' is even better with 12- to 18-inch yellow and green striped foliage. The flower stalks of this genus shoot skyward like rockets. They come early and stay a long time giving the plant a lot of garden interest.

Over the years I've collected a number of other cultivars of *Molinia caerulea* which I like very much. 'Sky Racer' is much bigger than the species, growing leaves to about three feet and flower stalks to nearly seven feet. With the early or late sun streaming through the flowerheads, it is spectacular. 'Tempest' is treasured for its very blue leaves while 'Moorflamme'(the bog fire) has purple-tinted leaves and dark inflorescence, and 'Moorhexe'(the bog witch) has straight dark stems and dark flowers.

There are so many wonderful grasses I have a hard time knowing where to stop. But perhaps we have covered enough for one month. Whether you're looking at grasses or conifers or broadleaf plants, take the time to look at the

Latin name and see if you can decipher the meaning. It will help you not only to learn your Latin, but also remember it.

Poaceae: Grasses Part II

I mentioned at the end of last month's column that there were so many wonderful grasses now available that I didn't know where to stop. In the hope that you too are, or are becoming interested in ornamental grasses, I thought we'd practice our Latin while looking at a few more genera in this wonderful family of plants. I'll stick with clump-forming grasses and avoid those that I've found to be invasive in my garden.

Panicum (PA-ni-kum) is the Latin name for the clump-forming switch grasses that made up a large part of the American tall-grass prairie. The species most commonly available today for our gardens is *P. virgatum* (vir-GAY-tum). The specific name, meaning twiggy, refers to the branching shape of the inflorescence. This adaptable grass prefers moist conditions in full sun, but will tolerate most any kind of soil (including our heavy clay) and will grow in dry or wet conditions. There are several notable cultivars. One is *P. v.* 'Haense Herms' (pronounced HEN-sa hairmz) which grows to a little over three feet with the flowers reaching another foot above the leaves. The foliage becomes increasingly red in the fall. Two other cultivars with colorful russet fall foliage are 'Rehbraun'(RAY-brown) and 'Rotstrahlbusch.' (ROTE-stral-bush). By the names I would suspect these were developed in Germany where much of the recent grass breeding has been done. 'Heavy Metal' is a American cultivar introduced by Kurt Bluemel in Maryland. It forms an upright clump of metallic blue foliage that turns yellow in the fall.

An outstanding cultivar of *Panicum virgatum*, in more ways than one, is 'Dallas Blues.' This is a much bigger plant, growing to five feet or more. What makes is so special is the very blue color of its foliage. The blooms which come late in the summer are reddish purple. Mine so far has stayed an upright clump without any staking or tying up. It offers the best of the colors of *Panicum virgatum* 'Shenandoah' and 'Prairie Sky'—other blue-foliaged, red-flowered cultivars—but makes a bigger impact with its size.

Some of the showiest flower heads in the Grass family belong to members of the genus *Pennisetum* (pen-ni-SEE-tum). Several species of these fountain grasses do well in our gardens. My favorite is *P. alopecuroides* (a-loh-pee-kur-OY-deez). Its quite a mouthful to say; but the *-oides* at the end of the word tells us it is like something else. In this case it is another grass called *Alopecurus* (a-loh-pee-KUR-us) the meadow-foxtail grass. Forming a neat mound of foliage about two and a half feet tall, the species produces its foxtail flowers in midsummer. This grass is happiest in moist, well-drained soil in full sun, but will tolerate less than perfect soil and some light shade.

My favorite cultivar is *P. a.* 'Hameln.' This is a very compact form with finely textured leaves and a soft mounded shape. Its creamy foxtail flowers come late in the summer and last through frost. It works well in the mixed border. There are two other cultivars worth mentioning: the black-flowering *P.a.* 'Moudry,' which has somewhat broader leaves, and 'Little Bunny,' a dwarf form that is a perfect addition to the rock garden.

Pennisetum caudatum (kaw-DAY-tum) closely resembles *P. alopecuroides*, but with white flowers. It may be that future botanists will decide it is a subspecies of the latter. Its name literally means having a tail and again refers to the tail-like flower heads.

One Pennisetum that prefers a lot of hot sun is *P. orientale* (or-ee-en-TAY-lee). Although the blossoms are smaller than those of other species, they come earlier and last longer. They also have a sort of pinkish color that blends well with flowers in the border.

Many of us have fallen under the spell of the burgundy beauty known as *Pennisetum setaceum* 'Rubrum' (se-TAY-see-um). Can you remember *setaceum* from an earlier column? It tells us that this plant is bristly. Sadly, this charmer is not hardy in my zone and so must be grown as an annual. Another non-hardy species worth growing as an annual, if you can find it, is *Pennisetum villosum* (vi-LOH-sum). It has another "hairy" name that describes the soft hairy nature of its flower heads. I grew this one for a summer and still have some of the old flower heads in a dried arrangement. They are really wonderful.

This past summer I discovered *Sesleria caerulea* (Sez-LAIR-ee-a se-REW-lee-a), a handsome compact evergreen grass that would make a nice edging plant. This blue moor grass grows about six to twelve inches and has two-toned leaves that are dark green on top and a sort of powdery white beneath. Named in honor of Leonardo Sesler, an 18ᵗʰ Century Venetian, who had a private botanical garden, it prefers moist, well-drained soil and will do poorly in overly dry areas.

No discussion of grasses for the small garden would be complete without mentioning the feather or needle grasses. The flowers of the genus *Stipa* are usually tipped with long needle-like awns that give the plants an airy, almost ethereal quality. *Stipa capillata* (STEE-pa ka-pi-LAY-ta) is a native of the dry grasslands of central Europe and therefore dislikes heavy wet soil and shade. But given sun and well-drained soil, it will make a statement planted alone or in a clump. Its narrow stiff leaves grow from one to two feet and are a nice gray-green color. In summer the flower stems rise another 18 to 24 inches above the foliage. Its name, again, refers to fine hairs and probably describes the flowers.

Stipa gigantea (jye-gan-TEE-a) is one of the showiest of the flowering grasses and makes an outstanding specimen plant. The feathery flowers float three or four feet above the two foot clump of foliage. This species blooms early with its flower spikes emerging in May and opening into loose open panicles in June. It is most effectively used as a tall accent plant in a place where the play of light and breezes can be appreciated.

Much smaller in scale and softer in appearance is the Mexican feather grass, *Stipa tenuissima* (ten-yew-ISS-i-ma). Although this has now been reclassified as *Nasella tenuissima* (na-SEL-la) since I wrote the column, its specific name refers to the extreme slenderness of the foliage. The nearly hair-like leaves grow to about 18 inches in a columnar clump. The flowers are bright green and turn to golden in the fall. Except for a dislike of wet feet, this grass is very adaptable to a variety of conditions. It survived in my perennial border through many wet winters. I get seedlings every year and although they have not been invasive, the potential for invasion may be there. Best to ask the experts in your area before planting it.

While visiting English gardens a couple of years ago, I was very much taken with *Stipa arundinacea* (a-run-din-AY-see-a). The name, as we learned last month, denotes a similarity to the reed *Arundinaria*. Although warned that it probably wasn't hardy in Portland, I couldn't resist bringing home some seeds. (Authorities variously rate this New Zealand grass as hardy from Zones 7 or 8 to

10, making it marginally hardy here.) In English gardens it makes a wonderful arching mound of foliage accented by flowers in panicles of purplish-green spikelets. Mine bloomed the second year and then became a real "thug." Although quite pretty this is probably one to avoid.

Another pair of beautiful, but aggressive (to be polite) grasses are the green and white variegated *Phalaris arundinacea*, (fa-LAIR-is) and velvet grass, *Holcus lanatus* 'Variegatus' (HOL-kus la-NAY-tus). These spread by root stolons and can take over a lot of your garden in only a season or two. A yellow-variegated form of *Bromus inermis* (BRO-mus in-ER-mis) is also a dangerous runner. Treat these running enchantresses with respect.

Although we learned some new Latin names this month, we also met some old friends from previous columns. Descriptions of color like *caerulea* are frequently repeated as are denotations of surface texture like hairiness *(setaceum, villosum,* and *capillata)*. Use the repetition of these and other Latin terms to make these names a working part of your gardening vocabulary. As you master some of the terms, you can begin to add new ones to your memory banks. By the way, two excellent books on grasses are John Greenlee's *Encyclopedia of Ornamental Grasses* and Rick Darke's *The Encyclopedia of Grasses for Livable Landscapes..*

Berberidaceae: Barberry Family

Since Oregon celebrates its birthday this month (February 14, 1859), it seems appropriate to take a look at our state flower *Mahonia aquifolium* (ma-HOH-nee-a a-qui-FOH-lee-um) and the family to which it belongs, the *Berberidaceae* (ber-ber-id-AY-see-ee). Although some botanists suggest that *Mahonia* should be grouped under the larger *Berberis* genus, it's still listed separately in the latest tome, *A to Z Encyclopedia of Garden Plants*, a joint publication of the American Horticulture Society and the Royal Horticultural Society.

I recently discovered the USDA website for native plants, http://plants.usda.gov. With either the common name or the scientific name you can call up the plant. If yours is an old name it will bring up the plant under the new name and show your name as a synonym. Often there are pictures that can help you identify our plant if you are unsure. This site maintains *Mahonia* as a separate genus. So, following these authorities, we will keep the two genera separate.

In general, plants in the *Berberidaceae* are herbs or shrubs native to the north temperate zone. A quick scan of the encyclopedias shows that most Barberry family members are native to Japan, China or North America. Their leaves are either radical (arising from the root or crown) or cauline (appearing on the stem), alternate, simple or compound. The flowers can be single or in racemes or panicles, are bisexual, and often have petals and sepals that are similar. The ovary is superior. Fruits can be berries or dry dehiscent seed capsules. Berries are fleshy or juicy fruits with one to many seeds; while a dry dehiscent fruit or seed capsule splits around its circumference along definite lines to release the seeds when ripe. Of the ten to twelve *genera* in the Barberry family (depending on which source you use), eight are native to North America including: *Achlys, Berberis, Caulophyllum, Diphylleia, Jeffersonia, Mahonia, Podophyllum* and *Vancouveria*. Not native to the U.S. are *Bongardia, Epimedium, Nandina,* and *Ranzania*. Let's start with a closer look at the American natives.

Achlys (AK-lis), whose common names are vanilla leaf or deer-foot, was named for a lesser Greek goddess of hidden places because it grows in wooded areas. Familiar to woodland walkers in the Pacific Northwest is *A. triphylla* (A. tri-FIL-a) or vanilla leaf. Its large fan-like, three-parted leaves are a common sight on both sides of the Cascades in the shady lowland forest understory from British Columbia to California. Both the leaves and flower stalks, which bear creamy spikes of petalless flowers, arise from a spreading underground stem.

I could find only one *Berberis* native to the United States, *Berberis canadense* (BER-ber-is ka-na-DEN-sa). A native of the Allegheny mountains from Virginia to Georgia and west to Missouri, it is deciduous, grows to six feet, has three-parted spines, two inch long spiny leaves, and racemes of bright yellow flowers followed by scarlet berries. It apparently is not as ornamental as the Asian species and is not grown for the trade. In fact, Michael Dirr, of the University of Georgia, doesn't even mention it in his *Manual of Woody Landscape Plants*. The barberries most often used in gardens come from Japan or China. They include the *B. thunbergii* (thun-BER-jee-eye) hybrids like 'Crimson Pygmy,' 'Aurea,' 'Bagtalle,' 'Rose Glow,' et al., from Japan, *B. julianae* (ju-lee-AN-ee) a yellow-flowered evergreen shrub from China, and others.

Caulophyllum thalictroides (kau-lo-FIL-um tha-lik-TROY-deez), blue cohosh, is a shade loving berberid native to the east coast from New Brunswick to Tennessee and South Carolina. Growing to about three feet, it has three-palmate leaves and yellow-brown to green-brown flowers that appear about the same time as the leaves in the spring. It's the bright blue seeds that give it its common name. The Latin name is derived from the Greek *kaulos* (stem) and *phyllon* (leaf). The plant's stem produces one stalk for each large leaf. *Thalictroides* denotes the similarity of its leaf to that of *Thalictrum* or meadow rue.

Diphylleia cymosa (die-fil-EE-ee-a sigh-MOH-sa) is the U.S. native of this small genus. Its habitat is in the moist shady woods of the southern Appalachians. The Latin name comes from its two leaves and its flowers in cymes (flower clusters that bloom from the center outward). The late summer flowers are white and are followed by blue berries on red stems. The common name, umbrella leaf, comes from the large size of its two deeply two-lobed leaves which can reach 16 inches.

Jeffersonia diphylla (je-fer-SO-nee-a di-FIL-a), commonly called twinleaf, grows from Ontario south through the Mississippi Valley to Alabama in moist woodland settings. This perennial is a clump-former with leaves deeply divided into two parts. Its white flowers appear on eight-inch stems in late spring or early summer. There is a lovely species from Japan called *J. dubia* (DEW-bee-a). The Latin means "doubtful" and refers to the lack of conformity in the pattern of its leaves which can be either rounded or kidney-shaped. The flowers of this Asian species are lavender and cup-shaped on dark stalks.

Podophyllum (poh-doh-FIL-um) is a genus of some nine species of rhizomatous perennials whose name literally means a plant with stout-stemmed leaves. To complicate matters slightly, *Stearn's Dictionary* explains the name is probably a contraction of *Anapodophyllum* from *anas* (duck), *podos* (foot) and *phyllon* (leaf) referring to the shape of the leaf. The American native is *P. peltatum* (pel-TAY-tum), the mayapple that is found throughout the eastern half of the country. It blooms in the spring hiding its solitary waxy white flowers beneath its large five-to nine-lobed leaves. After the flower a one- to two-inch, edible, egg-shaped greenish-yellow "apple" is produced.

Podophyllum hexandrum (hex-AN-drum) native to China and the Himalayas is quite similar except its large multi-lobed leaves bear purple markings. Its solitary white flowers are followed by large bright red fruit. *Hexandrum* refers to the six stamens in each flower.

Another species from China and Taiwan is *P. pleianthum* (plee-AN-thum). As its name from the Greek *pleios* (many) and *anthos* (flower) implies, it has multiple not solitary flowers. They are scarlet to purple and come in clusters of five to eight. Its huge shallowly-lobed leaves are glossy and make a real statement in the garden. The slightly smaller fruits are dark red. Recent introductions of *P. delavayi* (de-la-VAY-eye) are adding even more excitement to gardens. This species sports multicolored leaves that are real eye-catchers.

There are two west coast members of the family, *Mahonia* and *Vancouveria* that should be familiar to Northwest gardeners and walkers. Oregon's state flower is *Mahonia aquifolium* (ma-HOH-nee-a a-qui-FOL-ee-um) the tall Oregon grape. It normally grows to about five feet, has unbranched canes that produce glossy, compound, pinnate, holly-like leaves, and clusters of yellow flowers in early spring followed by edible blue berries. The genus was named for American horticulturist and author Bernard M'Mahon. *Aquifolium* was the classical name for holly so the plant was "M'Mahon's holly." The use of the classical name probably explains why the gender endings of the two names do not correspond as they do in the other species of the genus.

Mahonia nervosa (ner-VOH-sa) or Cascade Oregon grape is the other species we see most often in the Portland area. It is distinguished from *aquifolium* by its shorter stature (rarely above two feet) and its longer compound leaves that resemble a spiny feather. The leaves, arising from a basal rosette, grow to 12-inches or so and have 9 to 19 boldly veined holly-like leaflets. The yellow flowers are borne both in the leaf axils and at the tip of the stem. It is the bold veins in the leaf that give it the name *nervosa*.

In drier areas of Oregon two other varieties of *Mahonia* are found. Both are low-growing or creeping in habit. *M. repens* (RE-pens) is commonly found in eastern Oregon while the grayer-leaved *M. pumila* (PU-mi-la) occurs in southern Oregon.

A couple of species *M. lomariifolia* (loh-ma-ree-ee-FOL-ee-a) from China and *M. japonica* (ja-PON-i-ka) from Japan merit our attention as well. The former gets its name from a resemblance to *Lomaria,* now *Blechnum* (BLEK-num) a fern with narrow fronds that feature short, regular leaflets. Actually, we more often see hybrids from crosses of these two in garden use. Under the name *Mahonia x media* various cultivars such as 'Arthur Menzies,' 'Charity,' and 'Buckland,' are very garden-worthy plants. All form tall, vertical plants that feature terminal clusters of yellow flowers in racemes. Here in the Pacific Northwest, these cultivars bloom from late November into January providing not only color at an unusual time, but also a food source for our hardy Annas hummingbirds.

Vancouveria (van-koo-VE-ree-a) is native only to the United States and is found only in the area from Tacoma, Washington to northern California. It is closely related to *Epimedium*, a Eurasian genus, which it resembles. Hikers in our area will know *V. hexandra* (hex-AN-dra) the inside-out flower, also called duckfoot, that grows vigorously in moist, shady, open areas of the woods. Growing from creeping underground roots, it forms deciduous, duckfoot-shaped leaves in two sets of threes (twice ternate). The flower stalks are open panicles with numerous yellow or white flowers that appear to be inside-out because they are severely reflexed backward leaving the stamens and pistil exposed.

There are two evergreen forms of *Vancouveria* that grow mainly in south-

126

ern Oregon and northern California. *V. planipetala* (pla-ni-PE-ta-la) has flat-petalled, white flowers that are smaller than those of *V. hexandra*. The favorite of collectors, however, is *V. chrysantha* (kris-AN-tha), the yellow-flowered species. All of these make wonderful groundcovers in moist shady areas of your garden, particularly under shrubs like Rhododendrons.

Two non-native members of the Barberry family that are popular with gardeners are *Epimedium* (e-pi-MEE-dee-um) and *Nandina* (nan-DEE-na). There are some 30 to 40 species of *Epimedium* growing from the Mediterranean to temperate Asia. They generally have basal leaves that are bi- or tri-ternate, leathery, heart-shaped at the bases and pointed at the tips. Some species are deciduous while others retain their leaves until the new leaves appear in the spring. In garden situations, the leaves are generally cut back to the ground in late winter so that the flowers, which open just before the new leaves emerge, can be seen. The flowers are usually cupped or saucer-shaped and are often spurred. Colors range from white to yellow to pink, red or purple.

Epimediums are generally easy to grow and make wonderful groundcovers. Some of my favorites include *E. x versicolor* 'Neosulfureum' (ver-SI-kol-or neo-sul-FEUR-ee-um) with pale yellow flowers and sturdy mid-green leaves that turn rusty-rose in the fall, and *E. grandiflorum* (gran-di-FLO-rum), which has long spurs on the flowers. *Versicolor* means it is variously colored while *grandiflorum* is large flowered as most of you will remember. There are many cultivars of *E. grandiflorum* available in the market.

Another favorite is *E. x youngianum* (young-ee-AY-num) which is a cross between *E. grandiflorum* and *E. diphyllum* (dye-FIL-lum). There are numerous named cultivars of this cross all of which are a quite dainty. *Epimedium* is another genus that has been greatly expanded by recent plant collection in China. More and more varied species are becoming available to collectors and they are well worth the effort to find them.

No stranger to Northwest gardeners is *Nandina*, the final member of the Barberry family we'll discuss. This genus, whose name is a Latinization of *Nanten*, its Japanese name, has only one species, *N. domestica* (doe-MES-ti-ka). The specific name means the plant is frequently used in gardens, and that is certainly true in our area. If you were to look closely at the panicles of small white star-shaped flowers, you would surely see a resemblance to other flowers in this family, but even the pattern of leaf growth is remarkably like that of *Mahonia*. Growing on canes, the leaves are pinnate to 3-pinnate with lance-shaped leaflets. Like other members of the family, the evergreen leaves of this native of China, Japan and India often turn reddish in the fall and the red berries are delightful additions to winter arrangements.

Although the *Berberidaceae* is a relatively small family, it is full of good garden-worthy plants. Next time you are at a nursery or wandering around a garden, see how many of these Barberry family members you can find and check out the similarities.

Ranunculaceae: Buttercup Family

One of my favorite families for spring and summer flowers is the *Ranunculaceae* (ra-nun-kew-LAY-see-ee) or Buttercup family. This is a family of some 50 genera and about 1900 species of herbs and a few shrubs, most of which are native to the north temperate zone. Their leaves can be alternate or opposite; their flowers normally have two to many sepals and petals although the petals are sometimes absent. There are always many stamens prominently displayed. The fruit can be an achene (a small dry, indehiscent, one-seeded fruit with a tight skin), a follicle (a dry dehiscent fruit typically having more than one seed and opening along a line), or a berry. Members of this family include monkshood, baneberry, anemone, clematis, hellebores, delphiniums and larkspurs and are too numerous for us to cover in one column. So let's take a look at some of the spring bloomers of this genus.

Probably the earliest of the family to bloom in our area is *Eranthis hyemalis (*ee-RAN-this hye-e-MAY-lis), the winter aconite. This two-inch, single-flowered buttercup blooms in January here in the Northwest and its name tells us just that. *Eranthis* is from the Greek *er* (spring) and *anthos* (flower) and *hyemalis* is the Latin for winter flowering. *Eranthis* prefers alkaline soils and is therefore a little tricky to get established in our acid soil, but once settled in it will form happy colonies of bright yellow flowers. The foliage disappears as summer arrives so you should plant this in combination with other plants that will fill the summer holes.

The genus *Anemone* (a-NEM-oh-nee) offers a number of plants of garden interest. Experts are not certain of the derivation of the name. Some think it comes from the Greek *anemos* (wind) while others suspect it is a corrupted form of *Naaman,* another name for Adonis. His blood is said to have given rise to the red flowers of *Anemone coronaria* (ko-roh-NA-ree-a). Actually this erect perennial that arises from tubers comes in many colors and is quite showy. *Coronaria* literally means it was used to make garlands. A popular pair of *Anemone* species in woodland gardens in the spring are *A. blanda* (BLAN-da), meaning pleasing or charming, and *A. nemerosa* (ne-me-ROH-sa), of the woods. They make wonderful puddles of pastel color. My only caveat is that they are both empheral. They leaf out, bloom and then disappear. However, while you can't see them, they spread quickly on rhyzomaatous roots and can become difficult thugs.

The late summer- or fall-blooming anemones that include *A. x hybrida* (HYE-bri-da and *A. hupehensis* (hoo-pee-HEN-sis) are generally grouped as Japanese anemones. *Hupehensis* denotes the Hupeh region of China where this plant is found. The plants grouped under the x *hybrida* name are typically hybrids of the Chinese and Japanese anemones. These grow much taller, from two to six feet, and are stalwarts of the late summer garden. Once again, though beautiful in bloom, they can be quite aggressive.

We have several anemones native to the Columbia Gorge including: *A. deltoidea* (del-TOY-dee-a), the western white anemone, *A. lyallii* (ly-AL-lee-eye), the little mountain anemone, *A. multifida* (mul-TI-fi-da) the cliff anemone, and *A. oregana* (or-e-GAY-na), the blue-flowered Oregon anemone. *A. deltoidea* has single, white flowers rising above trifoliate leaves whose combined delta shape may give rise to the name. *A. lyallii* has a very pale small lavender flower and grows from a small tuber. *A. multifida* has pale yellow flowers and grows at high elevations in the cliffs. The name refers to its leaves which are finely divided. *A. oregana* has single blue flowers in early May. This is another species that spreads by underground runners.

A close relative of the anemone is *Pulsatilla* (pul-sa-TIL-la) or pasque flower. In fact, *Pulsatilla vulgaris* was once classified as *A. pulsatilla*. *Pulsatilla* comes from *pulso* (to strike or shake, as in the wind). The clump-forming *P. vulgaris* pushes very hairy shoots out of the ground in early spring. These open into anemone-like flowers and are followed by silky-haired seed heads reminiscent of clematis. With their many colors ranging from deep purple to red, pink and white, these are great additions to the rock or scree garden.

One of the sweetest members of the *Ranunculaceae* is the tiny *Anemonella* (a-ne-moh-NEL-la) or little anemone. The only species of the genus is *A.*

thalictroides (tha-lick-TROY-deez) commonly called rue anemone. It grows to only about three inches from tubers and has tiny pink or white flowers and leaves that resemble the *Thalictrum* which we'll discuss in a moment. Even cuter is the double form which is sold under several names including 'Oscar Shoaf,' 'Flore Pleno,' 'Shoaf's Double,' or 'Shoaf Pink.' *Anemonella* requires moist, fertile soil in a woodland sort of setting where it gets afternoon shade.

There is one spring-blooming *Thalictrum* (tha-LICK-trum) or meadow rue and several summer bloomers for your garden. The spring-bloomer is *T. aquilegiifolium* (a-kwi-lee-jee-i-FOL-ee-um). The generic name is the Greek name for this plant. *Aquilegiifolium* tells us that its leaves look like those of the columbine, *Aquilegia* (a-kwi-LEE-jee-a). In my garden, this *Thalictrum* is typically in bloom in May and June. It has blue-green leaves, grows to three feet, and is topped by a sea of fluffy pink, petalless staminate flowers which form flat, horizontal panicles.

We have a spring-blooming *Thalictrum* native to the Columbia Gorge. Although not as colorful as *T. aquilegiifolium*, *T. occidentale* (ok-si-den-TA-lee), the western mountain rue, has a certain ephemeral quality when it blooms in late April. Its leaves are much like those of *T. aquilegiifolium* and the staminate flowers are rusty and dangle in clusters from the terminal branches atop the one- to three-foot plants.

Some of the earliest perennials to bloom in my garden are members of the genus, Helleborus (hel-LE-bor-us), which was the Greek name for the Lent hellebore. *H. orientalis* (or-ee-en-TAY-lis), meaning from the east or from Asia, is native to Greece, Turkey and the Caucasus. This is the hellebore of our grandmother's garden with greenish-white, downward facing flowers. More and more these days the most common Lenten Rose we find is really *H. x hybridus*, the result of many crosses of *H. orientalis* with other hellebore species to improve color and the orientation of the blooms. The leaves are pedate and leathery, and either deciduous or over-wintering. You can now find hellebores with everything from yellow, to white, to pink, to dark red or nearly black blooms. These are amazingly hardy and dependable perennials that are tolerant of a wide range of soils, light and growing conditions.

H. x hybridus and *H. orientalis* are not the only garden-worthy hellebores. There are several species that prefer neutral to alkaline soils like the Corsican hellebore, *H. argutifolius* (ar-gute-i-FOL-i-us). Sometimes listed as *H. lividus ssp. corsicus* (LI-vi-dus), for its lead-colored or bluish-gray leaves, (KOR-si-cus), for where it grows. This is a much larger plant, growing up to 4 feet with biennial flowering stems. The flowers are pale green, pendent, smaller than those of *H. x hybridus*, and produced in terminal cymes. This species requires excellent drainage to thrive.

Another species that prefers dryer conditions is *H. foetidus* (FET-i-dus). *Foetidus*, as you may remember indicates something that smells bad, hence the common names of Stinking hellebore and Stinkwort in addition to Bear's Foot hellebore. This tall plant, growing to about 3 feet, has pedate leaves, that probably looked like bear tracks to some. In mid-winter, it produces large cymes of bell-shaped green flowers that often have red or purple margins. It's hard to find a more dependable perennial for mid-winter in to spring than hellebores.

The more you look at this family, the more you realize how many of our favorite flowers in encompasses. Next month we will take a look at some of the summer-blooming members of the Ranunculaceae.

Ranunculaceae Part II

Last time we took a look at some of the spring blooming members of the Buttercup family or *Ranunculaceae* (ra-nun-kew-LAY-see-ee). Let's now move the calendar ahead and see what this family offers for your summer garden.

Probably the earliest genus in the *Ranunculaceae* to bloom in summer my garden is *Aquilegia* (a-kwi-LEE-jee-a) or columbine. The name is derived from the Latin *Aquila* (eagle) because the flower's spurs resemble an eagle's talons. Although there are some wonderful species including some lovely alpines, the most common garden columbine is *A. vulgaris*. Through hybridization, both planned and accidental, this species comes in many colors, shapes and sizes. This is the columbine of your grandmother's garden.

Wildflower walkers will know our native species, *A. formosa* (for-MOH-sa) which frequents woods and thickets from Alaska to California and east into the Rocky Mountains. *Formosa* means beautiful and clearly fits this red-orange and yellow charmer. There is a pale yellow variety of this species that occurs naturally in the Blue Mountains of Oregon and east into the Rockies. It is *A. formosa* var. *flavescens* (flav-ESS-senz). *A. formosa* is quite similar to *A. canadensis* (kan-a-DEN-sis) which is probably familiar to readers east of the Rocky Mountains.

From Japan comes another easy to grow, yet smaller and more delicate species for your garden. It is *A. flabellata* (fla-bel-LAY-ta) which, as the name implies, opens like a fan. Growing to less than 12 inches, it has soft pale blue-purple flowers and bluish green foliage. It is happiest with some partial shade and moist soil.

Another plant from your grandmother's garden that's also a member of this family is the *Delphinium* (del-FIN-ee-um). The name comes from the Greek *Delphis* (dolphin) because someone thought the flowers resembled dolphins. We are most familiar with its showy hybrids like the statuesque Pacific Giants that the British seem to grow so much better than we do. (I understand the secret is manure and lime).

However, Peck's *A Manual of the Higher Plants of Oregon*, lists 28 native species of this genus. Five of those are native to the Columbia River Gorge. *D. burkei* (BUR-kee-eye) has finely cut leaves and produces purple blooms in June near Catherine Creek and in the McCall Nature Preserve. It grows from 10 to 20 inches tall. *D. menziesii* var. *pyramidale* (men-ZEE-zee-eye var. pir-a-mi-DAL-ee), whose name honors Archibald Menzies and describes its pyramidal shape, blooms in May near Rooster Rock and Multnomah Falls. Its purple blooms are held away from the stem by long pedicels or flower stalks giving it a looser, more open appearance.

Two more natives are named for English botanist Thomas Nuttall who visited the United States extensively between 1811 and 1834. *D. nuttallianum* (nut-tal-lee-AY-num) blooms in late April in the Tom McCall Reserve and other dry grass lands. Its height is 4 to 16 inches and the color bright blue. *D. nuttallii* (nut-TAL-ee-eye) is found in June on moist grassy slopes. It grows up to two feet tall and is dark blue.

D. trollifolium (troh-li-FOL-lee-um) obviously has leaves that look like a *Trollius* another member of the family. This poisonous delphinium is the tall dark purple species you find in the moist shady areas at lower elevations in the Gorge west of Bonneville in May. There is always a good stand where the trail crosses the creek on the way up to Angel's Rest.

For a full season of flowers *Cimicifuga* (si-mi-si-FEW-ga) has several species that bloom in the early, middle and late summer months. From the Latin *cimex* (bug) and *fugo* (repel) comes its common name bugbane. The first species to bloom in my garden is *C. racemosa* (ray-si-MOH-sa). Bearing its small white flowers in upright racemes, this east coast native blooms in June or early July. Its tall flower stalks can reach four or five feet rising from clumps of basal 2- or 3-ternate leaves. *Author's note: In the years since this column was written, the entire genus of* Cimicifuga *has been put into the genus* Actaea *(ak-TEE-a). The name comes from the Greek* aktea *meaning elder. Since not all growers have made the change, I've left the text as it was originally written.*

In late July or August *Cimicifuga ramosa* 'Brunette,' (ra-MOH-sa), which has luscious deep burgundy leaves and racemes of pinkish flowers, bursts into

134

bloom. *Ramosa* refers to the branching habit of this plant and is not a corruption of *racemosa* denoting the presence of racemes. (I should note that the nomenclature for cimicifugas is still under discussion and you might well purchase this one as *C. simplex* 'Brunette.') To date my Brunettes have grown to about three feet, somewhat shorter than the species. This is a perennial that is becoming more available at a reasonable price and it adds great foliage color to your garden.

Cimicifuga simplex 'White Pearl' holds off until September or October before it blooms, putting flowers into your garden when few things are blooming. The specific name means unbranched, just the opposite from *ramosa*. And, in fact, the plant puts numerous flower stalks up to a height of three to four feet directly from the clump of basal leaves. This species is native to northern Asia and is, therefore, quite hardy. All of these *Cimicifuga* species will take full sun if their feet stay cool and moist. But they will burn a bit if they get too hot so I plant mine where they'll be protected from the hottest afternoon sun.

We have a pair of native bugbanes that grow in the Gorge and on Mt. Hood. One is *C. elata* (ee-LAY-ta) that grows in the deep woods west of the Cascades and in the Gorge. As its name implies, it is a tall plant, reaching up to six or more feet. It can be found in the lower elevation forests and blooms in mid to late June in the Gorge. The other native is *C. laciniata* (la-sin-ee-AY-ta), the cut-leaf bugbane that grows at higher elevations in marshy areas or damp woods. It blooms in late August.

One member of the Buttercup family is grown more for its fruits than its flowers, although it is decidedly under-used in our gardens. I'm talking about *Actaea* (ak-TEE-a), the baneberry. The name is simply the ancient name for this plant. The white flowers of this perennial are arranged in spherical racemes and are not particularly showy. But the clumps of berries, either red or white depending upon the species, are wonderful. English gardeners are particularly fond of *A. alba* which they call "doll's eyes" because each white berry has a little black eye. *A. rubra* naturally has red berries; although, I have an *A. rubra* f. *neglecta* that has white berries. All are native to eastern North America and all make delightful accents in your garden.

I can't leave this wonderful family without mentioning one more genus that provides summer flowers for your garden. *Aconitum* (ak-oh-NYE-tum), with flowers that resemble hooded and spurless delphiniums, is a real show-stopper in your late summer or early fall garden. The name is once again the old Latin name for this plant whose common names describe its shape (monkshood) and its use as a poison (wolf's bane).

We most often see *A. carmichaelii* (kar-mye-KELL-ee-eye) in the nurseries. This Chinese species is named for Dr. J. R. Carmichael who was a medical man and plant explorer in China in the latter half of the 19th Century. It is a tall plant (to six feet) whose heavy, dark blue, delphinium-like spires open in September or October. There is a cultivar of this species called 'Arendsii' which grows a bit shorter.

For earlier color, look for *A. napellus* (na-PEL-us) which puts up its blue spears in mid-to late-summer. *Napellus* is a diminutive form of *napus* (little turnip) and refers to the tuber-like nature of the plant's root system. This species has some cultivars that offer some color variations. 'Albidum' (AL-bi-dum) has gray-white flowers and 'Carneum' (KAR-nee-um) has dusty pink blooms. Another early to midsummer bloomer is *A. henryi* 'Spark' (HEN-ree-eye), sometimes listed as *A.* 'Spark's Variety.' Mine grows to nearly five feet and has very deep blue-violet flowers throughout July and into August. *A. carmichaelii* and *A. henryi* are hardy in zones 3-7 while *napellus* is hardy in zones 5-8.

One species, *lycoctonum* (lye-KOK-to-num), whose name comes from the Greek *lykos* (wolf) and *ktonos* (murder), typically produces yellow flowers. Its subspecies, *vulparia (vul-PAR-ee-a)* is a wonderful petite form of this species. It stays at about 18 inches and has pale yellow blooms.

I expect you are beginning to appreciate my liking for the *Ranunculaceae*. Even after all I've written there are several wonderful genera untouched upon like *Clematis* (KLEM-a-tis). But I will save them for another time. Suffice it to say there are a great many garden-worthy perennials in the delightful Buttercup family.

136

Caprifoliaceae: the Honeysuckle Family Part I

In late July sitting on the terrace waiting for inspiration to strike, I found myself enjoying the fragrance of honeysuckle. I decided my muse had spoken and went to get my books to see what the Honeysuckle family or the *Caprifoliaceae* (kap-ri-foh-lee-AY-see-ee) includes. I found a number of familiar shrub *genera* and a few that are less well known. We'll begin with some that are familiar to most gardeners.

The *Caprifoliaceae*, literally the family of the goat leaf plants (a designation for which I can find no explanation), is commonly called the Honeysuckle family. Honeysuckle's botanical name is *Lonicera* (lo-NISS-er-a) and it is named for the early German botanist, Adam Lonitzer (1528-1586). In an earlier column we looked at some of the shrubby members of the genus in a discussion of fragrant winter-bloomers. One of those was *L. fragrantissima* (fray-gran-TISS-i-ma), the very fragrant deciduous shrub from China that bears creamy white flowers from winter into early spring.

Most of us are, perhaps, more familiar with the climbing members of the genus such as *L. japonica* (ja-PO-ni-ka) which is an invasive alien in gardens in the eastern and southern parts of the country. It does have some less invasive cultivars such as *L. j.* 'Aureoreticulata' (au-ree-oh-re-tik-yew-LAY-ta). Its leaves are netted with yellow lines as the name implies.

Another climber well known to visitors of English gardens is *L. periclymenum* (pe-ri-KLIM-en-um) whose specific name is the ancient Greek name for honeysuckle. The species has white to yellow flowers that are often flushed with red. Particularly good cultivars include 'Graham Thomas,' with white flowers turning yellow over a long period of time, and 'Serotina' (si-ROT-in-a) a Dutch hybrid whose white flowers are streaked with a dark purplish-red. Serotina literally means late and refers to the late bloom time of this cultivar. I have a cultivar named 'La Gasneria' whose purplish buds open into yellow flowers.

There are a number of shrubby loniceras native to the west coast. One is *L. involucrata* (in-voh-loo-KRAY-ta) or twinberry that is common from Mexico to Alaska. Its flowers and fruit come in pairs. The name *involucrata* refers to the presence of bracts that surround the tubular yellow flowers and later the black berries. These bracts start out green and turn red.

Lonicera conjugialis (kon-jew-gee-AY-lis), commonly called the wedded honeysuckle because its paired ovaries are not quite fused, grows in the high Cascade, Siskiyou and Blue Mountains of Oregon as well as in other western states. It produces small dark red flowers and dark red to nearly black berries. Two other natives are *L. ciliosa* (si-lee-OH-sa) which has small hairs on its leaf margins; and *L. hispidula* (his-PID-yew-la) which has bristly hairs on the underside of the style and filaments.

Another genus in the *Caprifoliaceae* familiar to Northwest gardeners is *Abelia* (a-BEE-lee-a), particularly *A. x grandiflora* (gran-di-FLO-ra). This mostly evergreen shrub with its arching branches of small, glossy leaves and terminal panicles of fragrant pink-white flowers is a common sight in our gardens. It is a cross between *A. chinensis* (chin-EN-sis) and *A. uniflora* (u-ni-FLO-ra). The genus gets is name from Dr. Clarke Abel (1780-1826), who traveled as a botanist with Lord Amherst to his embassy in Peking in 1816-1817. Faithful *Fearless Latin* readers will have no trouble with the specific names here. *Chinensis* means from China, *uniflora* indicates a single flower, and *grandiflora* means large-flowered. At one time this shrub was called *A. rupestris* (rew-PES-tris) meaning rock-loving.

The elderberry is yet another familiar member of this family. Here in Oregon we have three native elderberries: *Sambucus caerulea* (sam-BEW-kus se-REW-lee-a) the blue elderberry; *S. melanocarpa* (me-la-noh-KAR-pa) the black elderberry; and *S. callicarpa* (kal-li-KAR-pa) the red Pacific coast elderberry. The generic name is the old Latin one for this plant and may have derived from the Latin *sambuca* a kind of harp. The specific names describe the color of the berries. *Caerulea* means blue, *melanocarpa* is black, and *callicarpa* is simply a beautiful berry.

138

The elderberry most often used in our gardens is the European elder, *S. nigra* (NYE-gra) and its cultivars. Some of the best colored foliage for the back of mixed borders can be found with this species. For example, there are the dark red leaves of 'Guincho Purple,' the white-splashed leaves of 'Albopunctata' (al-boh-punk-TAY-ta), and the golden-edged leaves of 'Aureomarginata'(aw-ree-oh-mar-ji-NAY-ta). For a lacy texture you can also get 'Laciniata'(la-si-nee-AY-ta) which has very finely divided leaves.

There is also a European red elderberry, *S. racemosa* (race-e-MOH-sa). Some good cultivars of this elder are 'Plumosa Aurea'(plew-MOH-sa AW-ree-a) with finely divided golden foliage and 'Sutherland Gold' whose yellow leaf color lasts longer in the sunshine.

The final member of the family that widely known is the genus *Viburnum*. *Some* years ago this remarkable genus was the subject of a two-year study by GCA clubs. It is a large genus made up of some 225 species of shrubs native to America, Asia and Europe. The name is the ancient Latin name for one of its species. Descriptive specific names include: *acerifolium* (ay-se-ri-FOL-ee-um) "maple-leaved;" *fragrans* (FRAY-grans) "fragrant;" *macrocephalum* (mak-roh-SEF-a-lum) "larged-headed;" *plicatum* (pli-KAY-tum) "pleated," referring to the leaves; and *rhytidophyllum* (ri-ti-doh-FIL-um) "wrinkled-leaved." There are enough Viburnums to warrant a chapter all their own.

Caprifoliaceae Part II

Last time we looked at some members of the *Caprifoliaceae* or Honeysuckle family. I thought we would continue this time with a look at a few more members of the family. The first genus was quite popular a generation ago and then fell out of favor for a while. It is now gaining more acceptance again.

I am talking about *Weigela,* which is properly pronounced *(WYE-jee-la)* but is nearly always pronounced (wye-JEE-la). These deciduous shrubs were named for a German botany professor named Georg Wolfgang Weigel (1748-1831). Although there are some 12 species, we most often see *W. florida* (FLO-ri-da) and its cultivars. As its specific ephithet implies, this species is free-flowering when it blooms in late spring and early summer. The flowers are produced in corymbs, are funnel-shaped and typically darker pink to reddish outside and paler pink to white inside. A corymb, by way of review, is an inflorescence with a flat top in which the outer flowers open first.

Weigelas develop into moderately large shrubs (five to eight feet tall and wide). I confess to a very early dislike of genus because it was my job as a child to prune ours back into a reasonable size after it bloomed each summer. Having vowed never to have one in my own garden, I have recently put in a variegated form. It's not supposed to grow as tall as the species, going only to about four feet, and I do like the variegated leaves. Time will tell how long it stays. But my prejudices notwithstanding, it is a dependable shrub for the garden.

In bloom *Kolkwitzia amabilis* (kol-KWITZ-ee-a a-MAH-bi-lis), or beautybush, is strikingly similar to a weigela. Its pink bell-shaped flowers come in similar terminal corymbs. The flowers are a bit shorter than the weigela's funnel flowers and they have a yellow flush to their throats. But at a glance it's easy to confuse the two. This single-species genus was named for Richard Kolkwitz another German botany professor.

Symphoricarpos (sym-for-i-KAR-pohs), the snowberry, is probably more familiar to wildflower walkers than to gardeners in Portland. Its name, from the Greek *symphorein* (bear together) and *karpos* (fruit), alludes to its most visible feature, its clusters of berries. Most common in our area is *S. albus* found at low elevations in woods and thickets from British Columbia to California and across the continent. Although its pink bell-shaped flowers are small and often go unnoticed, its stunning clusters of snow white berries are eye-catchers.

There are two species found in Mexico. *S. microphyllus* (mye-kro-FIL-lus) is a shorter plant that produces semi-translucent pink or white berries. *S. orbiculatus* (or-bik-u-LAY-tus), which also grows in the eastern U.S., has rounder leaves, as the Latin name implies, and tiny pink-white flowers. Its fruit is dark purple-red, hence its common names coralberry or Indian currant. This is a genus grown for its fruit rather than its flowers.

Another member of this family is best known in its native area of the southeastern U.S. where it is called bush honeysuckle. This is *Diervilla* (dye-er-VIL-a), named for a French surgeon, M. Dierville, who introduced *D. lonicera* to European gardens in the early 18th Century. There are three species all native to the southeast: *D. lonicera* (lo-NISS-er-a), *D. rivularis (*riv-yew-LAR-is) and *D. sessilifolia (*ses-si-li-FOL-ee-a). All grow to about three feet and all have yellow flowers. Those of *D. lonicera* occur in the leaf axils whereas those of *D. rivularis* and *D. sessilifolia* occur in terminal clusters. *Rivularis* indicates a preference for growing near streams while *sessilifolia* describes the stalkless leaves.

The species usually found in gardens is *D. sessilifolia*. We planted some at Elk Rock a couple of years ago when we were looking for plants that could tolerate wet feet. We are still waiting for them to bloom. Maybe next summer.

My favorite member of this family is *Heptacodium miconioides* (hep-ta-KOH-dee-um mi-kon-ee-OY-dez). A Chinese shrub or small tree, it has been available for only the last eight or ten years. It's too new, in fact, to be in most books. Its common name, Seven-son flower, gives us a clue to its Latin name. *Hepta* means seven and *kodon* is Greek for bell. When the creamy flowers of this plant and its fruit fade away, dark reddish calyces persist looking like red bells. Presumably the specific name indicates the resemblance of this plant to *Miconia* (mi-KOH-nee-a), tropical trees and shrubs with showy foliage.

I love this plant for all the reasons described in its name. It has showy three- to four-inch leaves that unfurl in striking opposition along the branches. It has clusters (in sevens naturally) of creamy white flowers that start in early August and continue for many weeks, that are in turn followed by the persistent reddish calyces. An added bonus is the exfoliating bark reminiscent of crape myrtle. From a rather gangly adolescence, these shrubs grow to a handsome 15 or 20 feet in a short period of time. Mine went from four-inch pots in the fall of 1995 to 12 feet in about three years. This is an eye-catching shrub for anyone's garden. Its best feature perhaps is that it doesn't care what kind of soil it's planted in. It will do as well in gummy clay as it will in soil with the hard-to-find "perfect drainage," in full sun to considerable shade.

Moving from the lesser-known to the nearly-obscure, I found another member of the *Caprifoliaceae* that I have never seen in person but would love to see. This is *Dipelta* (dye-PEL-ta) with its "two shields" or shield-like bracts at the base of each flower. From the picture in the *A to Z Encyclopedia of Garden Plants* its leaves appear somewhat similar to *Heptacodium*. In general the genus has peeling bark, bell-shaped flowers and papery bracts that surround the fruit.

D. floribunda (flo-ri-BUN-da) produces many tubular flowers in terminal or axillary corymbs. These are pale pink marked with yellow. This species grows to 12 feet in zones 6-9. *D. yunnanensis* (yew-nan-EN-sis) has more arching stems, grows to about 10 feet and has white flowers marked with orange. It is hardy from zones 7-9. You have to wonder why this genus is so unknown in the trade. Dan Hinkley's Heronswood Nursery catalog for 2000 showed he has what he thinks is a form of *D. yunnanensis*. *Dipelta* seems to be new even to intrepid plantsmen like Hinkley.

The last member of this family is perhaps not truly hardy here without a special care in your garden, although I have seen it in English gardens. I am speaking about *Leycesteria* (lay-ses-TEER-ee-a) which was named for William Leycester, Chief Justice of Bengal about 1820. There is a species native to northern Burma and India that would be too tender for Portland gardens—*L. crocothyrsos* (kroe-ko-THIRS-os) that has saffron-colored flowers in a thyrse (a type of many-flowered inflorescence).

More hardy for us in the proper location is *L. formosa* (for-MOH-sa) meaning handsome. Commonly called the Himalayan honeysuckle, this upright, suckering shrub grows in canes sort of like bamboo. Its new shoots are an attractive blue-green. The leaves are opposite, tapered, dark green, and up to seven inches long. But it is the flowers the I love. They come in pendant spikes with tiers of white flowers partially covered with wine-red bracts. Very showy. Given the current trend in Portland gardening to test the boundaries of cultivation, this is a plant that would be fun to try. Perhaps the one caveat is that it is described as a thicket-forming, suckering shrub—that might be translated to invasive. But perhaps our zone 8 climate would control this shrub rated as hardy in zones 9 and 10. All in all the *Caprifoliaceae* has some lovely shrubs for our gardens. Next time you are nursery hopping look for some of them.

Lamiaceae: The Mint Family
Part I

In recent years I have become more and more interested in learning about plant families. I used to think knowing to which family a plant belonged was too much or unnecessary information, but I have since changed my mind. Knowing the families of the plants you grow or recognize gives you reference points when you come upon a plant that is new to you. Identification is easier when you compare what you see with what you know about plant families.

One of the eight families GCA has suggested for the 2001 and 2002 Plant Exchanges is the *Labiatae* (la-bee-AH-tee) or *Lamiaceae* (la-mee-AY-see-ee) commonly called the Mint family. Why, two family names? The first is the historic name for this family and is derived from the Latin *labiatus* meaning lipped. The plants in this family all have well-developed lips. *Lamiaceae* comes from the relatively recent decision to name plant families after a typical member of the family. In this case *Lamium* (LAY-mee-um). The family characteristic that is most easily identifiable, however, is that all members of the Mint family have square stems.

Depending on your source, the Mint family has about 180 genera and 3,500 species of herbs and shrubs. Although mints are found throughout the world, a great many come from the Mediterranean region. Their stems are usually square, their leaves four-ranked, simple, and often aromatic, and their lipped-flowers typically come in irregular cymes in the axils of bracts or leaves.

Without giving the familial relationship a thought, most of you are very familiar with some members of the Mint family because so many of them are often found in your herb gardens. Probably all of us with sufficient sun in our gardens have tried or currently grow lavender. Properly called *Lavandula* (la-VAN-du-la), the genus got its name from the Latin *lavo* (to wash) because it was so often used in soaps. The most common species grown is *L. angustifolia* (an-gus-ti-FOL-ee-a), the narrowed-leaved lavender, and its cultivars. The species grows to about three feet but a number of cultivars like 'Hidcote' are a bit smaller.

Lavandula x intermedia is a cross between *L. angustifolia* and *L. latifolia* (la-ti-FOL-ee-a), the spike lavender that has wide leaves and is a bit more compact. And *L. stoechas* (STEE-kas), the French lavender, has showy dark purple flowers topped by conspicuous purple bracts that look so stunning in dried arrangements. The name literally means "of the Stoechades," islands off the southern coast of France. Today these islands are known as the Isles d'Hyères.

The mint we love in our tea and battle in our gardens is another member of the family, *Mentha spicata* (MEN-tha spi-KAY-ta) or spearmint. Its name is one of the oldest known dating back perhaps 4000 years to the Greek *minthe* and Latin *mentha. Spicata*, of course means spike or spear.

Pennyroyal, often mentioned in English books, is *M. pulegium* (pooh-LEE-jee-um). It gets its name from the Latin *Pulex* meaning flea and it was thought to be a flea repellent. Peppermint, recognizable by its very dark, almost black, leaf color is *M. x piperita* (pi-per-EE-ta) which comes from the Greek word for pepper.

Oregano or marjoram is also a member of this family. *Origanum* (or-i-GAY-num) is the classical name for these herbs. The common names oregano and marjoram are hopelessly confused in this genus. What some call "oregano" others call "common marjoram." It must depend on whether one's lineage is Italian or northern European. The Latin for the common herb is *O. vulgare* (vul-GA-ree). This grows from 12 to 36 inches on woody-based stems and is hardy in zones 5-9. So called Sweet marjoram is *O. majorana* (may-jor-AY-na). This is indigenous to southwestern Europe and Turkey and grows to about 32 inches as a subshrub. It is hardy in zones 7-9.

There are several ornamental forms of *Origanum* including *O.* 'Kent Beauty' which is a prostrate, semi-evergreen subshrub with wonderful whorls of pink flowers throughout the summer. If grown in very well-drained soil, this lovely plant is hardy for us. Another ornamental oregano is *O.* 'Buckland.' It's an upright perennial about eight inches tall, with gray-green leaves and whorls of pink flowers in the summer that is hardy in zones 7-9.

Rosemary another herb garden favorite is also a member of the Mint family. *Rosmarinus* (rose-ma-RYE-nus) gets its name from the Latin *ros* (dew) and *marinus* (maritime) because in the wild it grows on the sea cliffs of southern Europe. The herb we are most familiar with is *R. officinalis* (oh-fi-si-NAH-lis). This specific epithet has historically been applied to plants used for medicinal and culinary purposes. Rosemary is increasingly hardy for us being hardy in zones 8-10. Global warming has made it a good perennial in my garden in recent years.

Salvia (SAL-vee-a), commonly called sage, is yet another stalwart in our herb gardens. Until fairly recently we mostly saw *Salvia officinalis* with a number of pretty colored-leaved varieties such as 'Tricolor.' Additionally, in our summer gardens we use *Salvia coccinea* (cock-SIN-nee-a), the bright red Texas sage, to lure hummingbirds and *Salvia farinacea* (far-in-AY-see-a) for its blue spires and gray-green foliage. *Farinacea* literally means mealy or flour-like and refers to the powdery or mealy stems. We treat both of these an annuals. In recent years salvias have become quite chic and we can now grow numerous species and varieties in a wide variety of colors and sizes. One thing they all have in a common is the need for well-drained soil.

One of my favorite herbs is summer savory. Its proper botanical name is *Satureja hortensis* (sat-yew-RAY-a hor-TEN-sis). The generic name is simply the ancient one for this herb, while the specific name means "of gardens." A native of southeastern Europe, summer savory is an annual for us. It has a hardier cousin, *S. montana* (mon-TAN-a) that, as the name implies, comes from the mountains that is hardy in zones 5-8.

Used more often as an aromatic edging to herb gardens than as a culinary herb is *Teucrium* (TEWK-ree-um) or germander. *T. chamaedrys* (ka-MEE-dris), named for a dwarf oak because if its short stature, is often used in this way. A native of Europe and southwest Asia it is perfectly hardy in our gardens. It has small, glossy, mostly evergreen leaves and produces pale pink or purple flowers in late summer or early autumn. The shrubby or tree germander is from the Mediterranean region. Properly *T. fruticans* FROO-ti-kans), meaning shrubby, it grows to a height of two to three feet with woolly-white stems, gray leaves and pale blue flowers.

As the old song tells us ..."savory, sage, rosemary and thyme"..., thyme is yet another member of the Mint family. There are some 350 species in this genus. Common garden thyme is, of course, *Thymus vulgaris* (TIME-us vul-GA-ris). This six- to twelve-inch subshrub has small, finely-haired, gray-green leaves which are very aromatic. The early summer flowers are pink or white and come in whorled racemes. This Mediterranean native is very hardy growing in zones 4-9.

A frequently used ornamental thyme is *T. serpyllum* (ser-PIL-lum). The specific name is the ancient Latin name for the genus. This is the mat-forming wild thyme or mother of thyme that works so well in rock gardens or cracks in stone walks and walls. It has numerous hybrids and cultivars such as 'Elfin,' 'Minimus,' and 'Minor' depicting size as well as many that demonstrate colors such as 'Aureus,' "Pink Chintz,' and 'Snowdrift.' Another favorite of herb gardeners is *Thymus x citriodorus* (sit-tree-oh-DOR-us) the lemon-scented thyme, which also comes in several colored-leaved cultivars.

I think it's very interesting that so many of our favorite herbs are all members of the same family, the *Lamiaceae* or *Labiatae*. There are some other members of this family that are good additions to both the herb and perennial garden which we will look at next month.

Lamiaceae: Part II

From cooking herbs to ornamentals the *Labiatae* or *Lamiaceae* has much to offer your garden. Last month we talked about members of the Mint family frequently used as cooking herbs. Other members of the family make ornamental additions to your gardens.

A popular ground cover is *Ajuga reptans* (a-JEW-ga REP-tans). Although the origin of the generic name is obscure, certainly *reptans* describes the creeping nature of this plant. The two-lipped tubular flowers of this species are typically dark blue and arranged in whorls at the leaf axils along the square stems. There are some interesting cultivars of *A. reptans* sporting colorful leaves such as 'Burgundy Glow' with wine red leaves and 'Multicolor' (sometimes called 'Rainbow') with green leaves marked with cream and rose. Another good species is *Ajuga pyramidalis* (pyr-a-mi-DAY-lis), named for its pyramidal flower stalks. A cultivar called 'Metallica Crispa' has tightly crinkled and curled iridescent purple-green leaves which look metallic in the sun.

Agastache (a-GAH-sta-kee) looks so much like salvia that it is often hard at first glance to tell them apart. Its name comes from the Greek *agan* (very much) and *stachy* (spike). These are natives of dry hilly areas in China, Japan, the U.S. and Mexico. Maybe one reason we are only beginning to see them in our nurseries is because they require that ever-difficult perfect drainage and full sun. Species found in the U.S. and Mexico include: *Agastache aurantiaca* (au-ran-TYE-a-ka) with orange flowers; *A. cana* (KAY-na), the hummingbird's mint; and *A. mexicanum* (mex-i-KAY-num), the Giant Mexican hyssop with edible rose-red flowers. There is a wrinkled-leaved species from China called *A. rugosa* (roo-GOH-sa) and a number of colorful cultivars such as 'Firebird' (copper-orange flowers), 'Tutti-Frutti' (raspberry-red flowers), and 'Pink Panther' (shell-pink flowers).

Many plants in the Mint family are sun-lovers so it's nice to come upon one like *Lamium* (LAY-mee-um) that prefers shade. Its name is simply the ancient one for this plant known commonly as Deadnettle. Probably the best species for your garden is *L. maculatum* (ma-kew-LAY-tum) or Spotted deadnettle, as its name implies. This rhizomatous perennial can be used much like *Pulmonaria* (pul-moh-NAY-ree-a) in shady areas as a low groundcover.

There are numerous cultivars such as *Lamium* 'Album' with white flowers and white spots on the leaves; 'Aureum' with yellow leaves having paler white centers and pink flowers; 'Beacon Silver' with pink flowers and silver leaves narrowly edged in white and 'Pink Pewter' with greenish-gray-edged, silver-gray leaves and clear pink flowers. One caveat is that this can be somewhat vigorous and may need to be kept in its place.

Monarda (moh-NAR-da) has been a garden favorite for centuries. Commonly called Bee balm because of its great attraction for bees, it was named after Spanish botanist Nicholas Monardes (1493-1588). *Monarda didyma* (DEE-di-ma) is the species most often used in gardens. Also known as Bergamot, it stands three to four feet tall and forms large clumps. The two-lipped flowers with their large reddish bracts are formed in two whorls at the top of the stems. With flower colors all in the pink to scarlet range, it is a magnet for hummingbirds as well.

Visitors to English gardens in June have long been wowed by the rows of *Nepeta* (NE-pe-ta) edging borders and walks with lovely blue spikes. *Nepeta cataria* (ka-TAR-ee-a) [of cats] is, of course, catnip. It stands about three feet and has aromatic leaves and hairy stems and purple-spotted white flowers in spike-like stalks. Most commonly used in gardens is the bi-specific cross *N.* x faassenii (fah-SEN-nee-eye), named for Dutch nurseryman H. J. Faassen, or one of its cultivars such as 'Dropmore' which has gray toothed leaves and large lavender flowers and 'Snowflake,' a low-grower with white flowers. Another garden favorite is *Nepeta* 'Six Hills Giant' that grows to about three feet with aromatic light gray leaves and very dark blue flowers.

For the late summer garden it is hard to beat the ghostly gray foliage and rich violet flowers of *Perovskia atriplicifolia* (pe-ROV-skee-a a-tri-pli-si-FOL-ee-a). That's a mouthful isn't it? To simplify, this Russian sage was named for a Russian general named V. A. Perovski (1794-c1857). The specific name means it has leaves like the salt bush, *Atriplex*. It prefers well-drained, rather poor soil in full sun and does well in alkaline and coastal soils. Maybe that is why I have never had any success with it in my acidic clay soil.

Another member of the *Lamiaceae* or *Labiatae*, with which I have been largely unsuccessful, is the Obedient plant, *Physostegia virginiana* (fye-zoh-STEE-jee-a vir-jin-ee-AY-na), The name describes the inflated calyx that covers its fruit from the Greek *Physa* (bladder) and *Stege* (covering). It is native to the east coast and hence "of Virginia." Cultivation instructions call for fertile, moist soil in sun or partial shade. It's disappointing that I can't seem to grow this lovely cutting flower because as a child I loved to make the rows of flowers "obey" as I moved them around the stem. The blossom colors range from purple to pink to white on 12- to 24-inch stems.

With very few exceptions I do not plant annuals in my garden as I do not have enough of the hot sun they crave. But this year with a Labor Day weekend wedding, I was desperate to keep the garden colorful late into the season. So I succumbed to the brightly colorful leaves of *Coleus* (KOH-lee-us) in late July. Frankly, I had never thought about what family *Coleus* was in. It is, of course, a member of the Mint family but it has a new name. It is now grouped under the genus *Solenostemon* (soh-len-OS-tee-mon) which probably refers to its pipe-shaped stamens. But you don't grow this plant for its flowers. It's the leaves that excite and it does tolerate considerable shade.

What we purchase as "Coleus" are cultivars of *Solenostemon scutellarioides* (SKOO-te-lar-ee-OY-deez) which is named for its resemblance to another member of the family, *Scutellaria* (Skoo-te-LAY-ree-a). In its native Malaysia it is a perennial. When you study the shape of the leaves and flowers, it is not hard to see the resemblance to salvia and other members of the family.

We have covered a lot of Mint family plants in this and the last column without covering all of the genera. But before we end our discussion of this family, there is one more genus which is deserving of a place in your garden. This is *Stachys* (STA-kis). The Greek name refers to the spiked flower stalks. *Stachys byzantine* (by-zan-TEE-na), is also known as *S. lanata* (la-NAY-ta) meaning woolly which describes the wonderfully woolly leaves and stems of this plant. It's primarily planted for its hairy gray leaves and many gardeners remove the blossom stalks before they open so they will not detract from the gray foliage. *Byzantine* tells us where this plant was first found. This is the Lamb's ears or Woolly betony we all love.

There are, however, other garden-worthy species of this plant including *S. macrantha* (ma-KRAN-tha) or big-flowered stachys that has rosettes of broadly ovate, crinkled, dark green leaves and rosy-red flowers. I have an adorable little species in my rock garden called *S. densiflora* (den-si-FLO-ra) which has dense heads of white flowers and rosettes of crinkled leaves.

As I was editing this column, I belatedly decided to take a look in Peck's *A Manual of the Higher Plants of Oregon* to see what members of the family are native to Oregon. I found we have quite a few natives and some introductions from Europe that have naturalized themselves. We have, for example, *Teucrium occidentale* (TOO-kree-um ox-si-den-TAY-lee) or Western germander which is found in wet ground east of the Cascades. We also have a number of *Scutellaria* species which are commonly called Skullcaps. Eastern Oregon has a couple of native giant hyssops: *Agastache urticifolia* (ur-ti-si-FOL-ee-a) in dry wooded areas and *A. cusickii* (koo-SIK-ee-eye) in the Steens.

Several species of *stachys* are found on both sides of the Cascades principally in wet areas. They include: *S. ciliata* (si-lee-AY-ta) [fringed with hairs], the Great hedge nettle; *S. emersonii* (em-er-SON-ee-eye) Emerson's hedge nettle; and *S. rigida* (RI-ji-da) the Rigid hedge nettle.

The Stinging nettle, *Urtica dioica* (UR-ti-ka dee-oh-EE-ka) incidentally belongs to its own family, the *Urticaceae* (ur-ti-KAY-see-ee). Its leaves resemble those of the Mint family, but it has neither the square stems nor the two-lipped flowers. *Dioica* indicates that the plant is dioecious - having male and female reproductive parts in separate plants.

I could to on and on, but I won't. Suffice it to say there are a number of Mint family members native to Oregon. The Mint family is one rich in aromatic plants for your table and your garden. They are recognizable by their square stems, their two-lipped flowers usually in whorls in the leaf axils, and their opposite and aromatic leaves. Now that you have been introduced, see how many you can identify when you are plant hunting or garden touring.

Amaryllidace: Amaryllis Family

The *Amaryllidaceae* (a-ma-ril-lid-AY-see-ee) or Amaryllis family is so closely related to the *Liliaceae* (li-lee-AY-see-ee) that some genera have been moved from one to the other several times, and lily appears in many of the common names. Members of the family are monocots, meaning that they put up a single grass-like leaf from seed. They grow from tunicate bulbs or corms—rarely from rhizomes. The trunicate bulbs are enclosed in a "tunic" like that of an onion or a daffodil. The leaves are normally basal; the flowers terminal and either single or many in umbels. How the flowers are attached to the umbels determines whether a plant is a lily or an amaryllis.

This is a large family found primarily in the warm temperate regions of South America, South Africa and the Mediterranean. Although many of these showy bulbs are not hardy in our gardens, some are popular pot plants like *Clivia* (KLYE-vee-a) and *Hippeastrum* (hip-pee-AS-trum).

Hippeastrum is the common Amaryllis you buy in a box and just add water to. The name comes from the Greek *Hippos* (horse) or *Hippeus* (rider). Experts debate whether the allusion has to do with the appearance of a horse's head at a particular stage in the blossom's development or whether it was suggested by the name given a species—*equestre* (belonging to a horseman). What we are most familiar with are large-flowered hybrids.

Clivia miniata (mi-nee-AY-ta) is one of my favorite houseplants. The specific name aptly describes its cinnabar-red flower color while the generic name honors Lady Charlotte Clive, Duchess of Northumberland and granddaughter of Robert Clive. A native of South Africa, it has fabulous strappy, evergreen leaves and large umbels of orange-red flowers. I can get two bloom periods a year (one around January and one in mid-summer) if I withhold water during October and November and then move the plants to the shaded patio (any sun will burn the leaves) in May. In between, if I'm lucky, I get multi-headed clumps of bright red fruit. The plant blooms best when its roots are restricted. So don't transplant your *Clivia* until it breaks its existing pot. Much hoopla has been made about a yellow-flowered variety. Mrs. Lamont DuPont Copeland, a member of the Garden Club of Wilmington (Del), had one of the first of these much sought-after plants and she generated frenzied bidding offering pieces of it at a local Rare Plant Auction several years running. These yellow beauties are now becoming generally available at reasonable prices.

There are several genera in the family that are hardy in our gardens. One is *Amaryllis* (a-ma-RIL-iss), named for the beautiful shepherdess of classical poetry. It has only one species *A. belladonna* (bel-la-DON-a). Commonly called Naked Lady, Magic lily, or Resurrection lily, this bulb from South Africa, hardy in zones 7-10, blooms in the fall in Portland gardens. It sprouts heavy strap-like leaves in the very early spring that die away long before the naked flower stalks bearing rose-pink flowers appear in the fall.

There may be only one species of *Amaryllis*, but there are 130 species of *Crinum* (KRY-num) whose name comes from the Greek *Krinon* (a kind of lily). We can grow *C. asiaticum* (ay-zee-A-ti-kum) also known as Poison bulb. This native of tropical southeast Asia forms a tall deciduous clump that produces umbels with up to 20 narrow-petalled, fragrant, white, lily-like flowers in the spring and summer. We should also to be able to grow the hybrid *Crinum x powellii* (pow-ELL-ee-eye) also hardy in zones 7-10. This hybrid cross of two species grows to five feet with medium-pink flowers from late summer to autumn. It's best grown in moist, deep, humus-rich soil in full

One of the earliest of the spring bulbs to bloom is *Galanthus nivalis* (ga-LAN-thus ni-VA-lis) or Snowdrop. The name tells us both its color and its preferred growing conditions. *Galanthus* comes from the Greek *gala* (milk) and *anthos* (flower) and alludes to the milk-white blooms. *Nivalis* means snow-white and growing near the snow. It is native from the Pyrenees to the Ukraine and grows about four inches tall. It is recognized by its drooping white flowers with an inverted "v" of green at the tip of each inner tepal and its honey-like smell. A taller snowdrop is *G. elwesii* (el-WE-zee-eye) named after a botanist, Elwes. This giant snowdrop has broader leaves that can be sort of twisted and white flowers which sometimes develop greenish markings on the inner tepals.

The spring-blooming *Leucojum vernum* (lew-KOH-jum VER-num) is often confused with *Galanthus* species. It too blooms in the early spring and has white drooping bell-like blossoms that have green markings on them. But the bells are shorter and more open, and the green markings are on the tips of each petal. The specific name of this native of southern Europe literally means spring-time and the generic name comes from the Greek name for another white flower, *leukon ion*, the white violet.

Leucojums aren't just spring flowers, however. There is a summer snow-flake, *Leucojum aestivum* (es-TYE-vum) that produces small bell-shaped, green-tipped, white flowers on leafless stalks in late spring to early summer. This plant is native in Great Britain and central Europe into Turkey and the Ukraine. There is also a fall-blooming snowflake, *L. autumnale* (au-tum-NAH-lee). This plant has grassier leaves and small white drooping flowers with red-tinged bases. It's found naturally in southwestern Europe and North Africa.

Lycoris (lye-KOR-is), the spider lily, gets its name from a mistress of Mark Antony who was known for her intrigues. The most hardy species is *L. squamigera* (squaw-MI-je-ra) or Resurrection lily (zones 6-10). The name means scaly and possibly describes its bulb. As with the *Amaryllis*, this bulb puts up leaves in the spring that die away to be followed in midsummer by 18-28 inch flower stalks bearing up to eight rosy-red, somewhat wavy flowers in umbels. They get their spidery appearance from the long stamens that protrude well beyond the petals.

Another popular species is *Lycoris radiata* (ray-dee-AY-ta), the Red spi-der lily. It gets its name from the long, radiating stamens that stick out well beyond the reflexing tepals. A native of Japan and hardy in Zones 8-10, it nor-mally blooms in late summer or early fall. The Golden spider lily, *L. aurea* (AU-ree-a) is a native of China and Japan and is also hardy in Zones 8-10. Both of these species grow to about 24 inches.

From South Africa comes another delightful bulb named after the sea nymph *Nerine* (ne-REE-nee). These grow naturally in well-drained areas like mountain screes and on rock ledges. Most seem to be hardy in Zones 8-10. There are numerous large-flowered hybrids, but I suspect I would go for the smaller-flowered species in my garden. For example, there is *N. filifolia* (fi-li-FOL-ee-a) with grassy eight-inch leaves and umbels of small bright pink to white flowers in autumn. It is nearly evergreen, producing new leaves as the old ones fade away.

Nerine flexuosa (flecks-yew-OH-sa) has strappy leaves about 12 inches tall. In late fall it produces compact umbels with from 10-20 dark-veined, pink flowers with wavy margins. *Flexuosa* means wavy or zig zag.

N. sarniensis (sar-nee-EN-sis) from ancient Sarnia, now Guernsey, makes bright orange-red compact flower heads in early autumn. With its tepals greatly reflexed, its protruding stamens give this bulb an explosive appearance.

While I have only touched the surface of this large family, I will finish this discussion with one last, greatly underused genus, *Sternbergia* (stern-BER-jee-a). This winter daffodil (which really looks more like a crocus) was named for Count Kaspar M. von Sternberg (1761-1838), an Austrian clergyman and scientist who founded the Bohemian National Museum in Prague. A patch of *Sternbergia lutea* (LEW-tee-a) in full bloom at Longwood Gardens when I visited in early October really caught my attention. It has bright daffodil-yellow, goblet-shaped flowers and narrow, daffodil-like leaves. What a cheery sight at the onset of autumn!

S. candida (KAN-di-da), from Turkey, has sparkling white flowers as its name implies. *S. clusiana* (klew-zee-AY-na), named for Carolus Clusius, a Latinization of Charles de l'Ecluse, is sometimes called *S. macrantha* (ma-KRAN-tha) for its large (three-inch) funnel-shaped yellow flowers. This genus is a "must" when you make your next bulb order. Spring is full of bulbs, but the fall...what better time to enjoy the colors of spring again?

Are you excited about this large family of bulbs? I hope I have at least gotten you thinking about adding some of them to your gardens. I should also mention before we leave the *Amaryllidaceae* that the genus *Narcissus* (nar-SIS-sus) is also a member of this family. It is worthy of a column all by itself, and I did, in fact, devote a column to *Narcissus* which appears in a later chapter. Keep your eyes open for some of these bulbous perennials at your favorite nurseries.

Araceae: Arum Family Part I

For the next couple of months I want to continue our look at plant families and highlight the *Araceae* or Arum family. It's a diverse family of some 40 genera, many of which are native to tropical climes. The most recognizable feature of an aroid is its inflorescence that typically consists of a multi-flowered spadix (a club-like spike) surrounded by a leaf- or bract-like spathe. The flower of Skunk cabbage is a perfect example. This month I want to look at just one genus in the *Araceae* because its popularity has skyrocketed in recent years. That genus is *Arisaema* (a-ri-SEE-ma) whose name from the Greek *Aron* (arum) and *Haema* (blood) literally means "of the arum family." Just a few years ago you were lucky to find two or three species listed for sale. Today you can easily find a dozen or more species in catalogs and at plant sales. I remember Dan Hinkkey once offering 24 different Arisaemas in his Heronswood catalog

Most of the species available today are native to China, Japan, the Himalayas and North America and, except for the North American species (Zones 4-9), are hardy in Zones 6 or 7 through 9. Our American Jack-in-the-pulpits are pretty tame when compared to their Asian cousins. *Arisaema triphyllum* (try-FIL-um) has one to two leaves on 6- to 24-inch stems, that are divided into three leaflets, from whence the name. The greenish spadix is contained inside a hooded green spathe during the spring and early summer. Bright red berries cluster at the top of the stem in the fall. *A. dracontium* (dra-KON-tee-um), also known as Dragon root, is much like *A. triphyllum* but with a many-segmented leaf, a shorter flower stem and a longer spadix.

While the American Arisaemas are cute, the Asian ones are wild, almost reptilian. People either love them or hate them, but no one ignores them. One of my favorites is *Arisaema sikokianum* (si-koh-kee-AY-num) which is named for the island of Shikoku in southern Japan. Growing to nearly two feet, it has two pedate leaves (*palmate leaves in which the basal lobes or leaflets are also lobed*), one with three lobes and one with five. Sometimes the leaves are variegated with silver. The flower, a deep brown spathe striped with white, with a pure white spadix, looks sort of like an exotic jack-in-the-box.

The name of *Arisaema candidissiumum* (kan-di-DIS-si-mum) somewhat overstates its pure whiteness, as its spathe is white with pink stripes. But it is a winner nonetheless. The fragrant blossom stalk appears before the solitary three-palmate leaf in early summer. Growing to about 16 inches, this species is native to western China.

From the Himalayas we get some truly reptilian species. *Arisaema consanguineum* (kon-san-GWIN-ee-um) looks a bit like a cobra hiding under an umbrella with its hooded white, green and brown striped spathe situated below its single, but much-divided leaf. Its specific name literally means "related" but to what I can't say. This is a tall plant reaching nearly three feet.

Another snake-like species from the Himalayas is *A. griffithii* (grif-FITH-ee-eye) named for William Griffith (1810-1845) a British botanist who collected in India and Afghanistan. Beneath two large leaves that are divided into three diamonds, it produces a purple and green, heavily striped and hooded spathe. You almost have to lift the leaves to see the flower close to the ground on this two-foot plant.

A. jacquemontii (jack-MON-tee-eye), named for Victor Jacquemont (1801-1832), a French naturalist, somewhat resembles our native *A. triphyllum* with its green and white-striped spathe. But this Himalayan native bears its flowers above its leaves. These leaves are palmate and are divided into three to nine lance-shaped leaflets.

Arisaema ringens (RING-ens) is a favorite of mine. Its large, hooded green and purple-striped spathe rises from the ground like a cobra. The gaping purple lips of the spathe give it the name *ringens* which means gaping. This is one you have to see as my description doesn't do it justice.

Some Arisaemas have long thread-like extensions from the hoods of their spathes that are used to lure and transport insects for fertilization purposes. *A. costatum* (ko-STAY-tum) is one such species. Native to Nepal, this plant gets its name from the "ribbed" appearance of its spathe which is hooded, deep purple-brown, and striped with white. A long red thread extends from the curved hood of its spathe. Its picture in the *A to Z Encyclopedia of Garden Plants* looks like three red cobra-like snakes having a meeting.

As I mentioned before, Arisaemas are not for everyone, at least not at first meeting. But given time they grow on you, and they will most certainly give visitors to your garden something to talk about. All those mentioned here are hardy in our gardens and most are available in the trade. They prefer shade to part shade, and moist but well-drained, humus-rich, neutral to acidic soil. Seek them out and add some exciting wildlife to your garden.

Araceae Part II

Last month we looked at the genus *Arisaema* (a-ri- SEE-ma), one member of the *Araceae* or Arum family. This month let's look at some other aroids. In this rather diverse family, that includes terrestrial, aquatic and epiphytic plants, it's the inflorescence that combines a spadix and a surrounding spathe that set aroids apart.

Many members of this family are native to the tropics and suitable for use in our area only as houseplants or as summer annuals. We are all familiar, I'm sure, with *Dieffenbachia* (dee-fen-BACH-ee-a) and *Philodendron* (fi-loh-DEN-dron) but probably don't think of them as aroids because we don't see them blossom.

Dieffenbachia is an oft-used house plant, commonly called Dumb-cane because its sap is supposed to render one unable to talk. It was named for J. F. Dieffenbach (1790-1863), who was the gardener at Schönbrunn palace in Vienna in about 1830. Most of the plants we see are cultivars of *D. seguine* (se-GEE-ne) usually sold under the name *D. maculata* (ma-kew-LAY-ta) which means spotted and refers to the coloration of the leaves. It's grown for its leaves not for the seldom-seen flowers.

Philodendrons are also tropical plants grown for their leaves. They are native to Florida, Mexico, the West Indies and tropical South America. The generic name comes from the Greek *phileo* (to love) and *dendron* (a tree) and refers to the tree-climbing habit of some species. One of the most common species is *Philodendron scandens* (SKAN-dens) the Heart-leaf or Sweetheart plant. It's a climber, as its name implies, with leathery green heart-shaped leaves. Easy to grow, it's frequently the plant of choice for novice growers and college students. If your's were to blossom, it would have green spathes that are white inside.

There are also tree-like philodendrons that are used as house plants. *P.*

bipinnatifidum (bye-pi-na-ti-FOL-ee-um) is a non-climbing plant that can grow to 15 feet in its native Brazil. It has long-stalked leaves that are typically heart-shaped and bipinnate or doubly pinnate. A leaf is said to be pinnate when its leaflets are arranged like a feather. It's doubly pinnate or bi-pinnate when the leaflets themselves are arranged like a feather.

Spathiphyllum (spa-thi-FIL-um) is another familiar tender aroid used as a house plant. But this one blooms regularly in cultivation. The name, from the Greek, refers to its leaf-like spathe. The species most often seen is *S. wallisii* (wa-LIS-see-eye), named for Gustav Wallis who introduced it to the trade. It's a rhizomatous perennial, native to Columbia, Costa Rica, Panama and Venezuela, with wavy-edged, oblong dark green leaves. The flowers consist of fragrant white spathes surrounding green and white spadices. The cultivar *S.* 'Mauna Loa' is a larger plant with a wide open oval spathe.

One of the more exotic aroids is the bright red *Anthurium andraeanum* (an-THUR-ree-um an-drey-AY-num) commonly called Flamingo lily, Tail flower or Painter's palette. Its name comes from the Greek *anthos* (flower) and *oura* (tail) referring to the tail-like spadix so visible against the red spathe. *Andraeanum* honors Edouard Francis André (1840-1911). The leaves are arrow-shaped and shiny and the spathes are bright red, heart-shaped, and often puckered. The spadix is yellow.

Long before tropicals became the "in" plants for our gardens, southerners were growing *Caladium* (ka-LAY-dee-um) in their shade gardens for its showy leaves. The name is the Latinized form of *kaladi* a Malaysian plant. Its long peltate leaves *(having the leaf stalk attached near the middle of the leaf)* are shield-shaped and typically streaked or spotted with red, pink or white. Their requirement of high humidity makes them better suited to steamier parts of the country than Oregon.

The popularity of tropicals has increased the use in Oregon gardens of two genera related to *Caladium, Alocasia* (a-loh-KAY-see-a), Elephant's ears, and *Colocasia* (koh-loh-KAY-see-a), taro. *Colocasia* is from the Greek *kolokasia*, the name for the root of another plant. *Alocasia*, meaning "not *Colocasia*," refers to the separation of these two closely related genera.

Colocasia is widely grown as a staple food in warm climates as it prefers a swampy, moist habitat. The leaves are large and arrow-shaped with prominent veins. Although it rarely flowers in cultivation, in the wild it produces small white spathes with spadices that develop single-seeded green berries. It's used in summer bog or water gardens where its large leaves add interesting texture.

Alocasia also prefers damp soil and has insignificant flowers that are followed by clusters of red or orange fruits. They are grown for their large leaves that are very prominently veined and often streaked with black, bronze or dark violet. *A. macrorrhiza* (mak-roh-RYE-za) has a large root, as the name implies, but also very large, plain green leaves that can up to three or four feet long. The root is edible.

A. cuprea (KOO-pree-a), meaning coppery, has 18-inch leaves and dark green zones and midribs with copper-colored zones in between. The undersides of the leaves are red-violet. *A. plumbea* (PLUM-bee-a), meaning relating to lead, has huge dark purplish-green stems and leaves with wavy margins, purple veins and silver undersides. These are all natives of Indonesia and Asia.

There are a few members of the family that are hardy in our climate. One is even a native. *Lysichiton americanus* (li-si-KYE-ton a-me-ri-KAY-nus) is our locally native Skunk cabbage. The name comes from the Greek *lysis* (a loosening or releasing) and *chiton* (a cloak) and refers to the releasing of the spathe from the spadix as the fruit ripens. The bright yellow spathes and the huge green leaves of these wet ground lovers are a sure sign of spring in the northwest. The white blooming form from NE Asia, *L. camtchatcensis* (kamt-shat-CEN-sis) is highly prized in many European gardens. Incidently, the Skunk cabbage of eastern North America, which has a much more prominent skunk aroma, is another member of the family, *Symplocarpus foetidus* (sim-ploh-KAR-pus FE-ti-dus). The name refers to the combining of the ovaries to make a single fruit from the Greek *symploke* (a connection) and *karpos* (fruit).

Arum (AIR-um), the genus that gives the family its name, has several species hardy in our climate. *A. italicum* (i-TAL-ik-um) is highly touted for its arrow-shaped, white-veined leaves and showy clusters of bright orange fruit. It has been such an invasive weed in my garden for the past 30 years that I can't find a single nice thing to say about it. So I'll go on to some that may be less problematic.

A. creticum (KRE-ti-kum) from Crete has bright yellow spathes that curve back to reveal the fragrant yellow spadices. It has unmottled green, arrow-shaped leaves. *A. dioscoridis* (dio-SKO-ri-dis) seems to be named for an early Greek physician, Pedanios Dioscorides who compiled *Materia Medica* an important work on medical herbs in the 1st century. It's described as having purple or pale green spathes spotted with maroon-purple and narrow leaves.

Another aroid that's hardy for us is *Acorus calamus* (A-ko-rus KA-la-mus) commonly called Sweet flag. Just to confuse things, *Acorus* is also the Latin name for the iris *I. pseudacorus* (sood-A-ko-rus). *Calamus*, from the Greek *kalamos* (a reed), refers to the narrow foliage. This plant, and especially the variegated form, is used primarily for its upright foliage in moist situations. Mine has never bloomed but it's said to produce two- to three-inch, horn-shaped flowers in the summer.

Calla lilies are also members of the *Araceae* but are not of the genus by that name. There is only one species of the genus *Calla* (KAL-la) and that is *C. palustris* (pa-LUS-tris) which, as the name implies, grows in bogs in Europe, Asia and North America. It has heart-shaped leaves about eight inches long, and white-spathed flowers followed by dull red berries in the fall.

What we think of as Calla lilies are members of the genus *Zantedeschia* (zan-te-DESH-ee-a), named for Francesco Zantedeschia, a 19th century Italian botanist. Most of our callas are cultivars of the species *aethiopica* (ee-thee-OH-pi-ka) that is native to Africa. These rhizomatous perennials can be grown either in moist ground or in standing water. In early September these grow like weeds throughout the southern tip of South Africa. Certainly preferable to dandelions to my mind.

I can't leave the Arum family without at least mentioning a couple of odd members of the group. One is *Dracunculus vulgaris* (dra-KUN-kew-lus vul-GA-ris) or Dragon arum. It produces rather large, foul-smelling maroon spathes with dark maroon to nearly black spadices. It was thought to be a "naughty" plant by Victorians who attached sexual overtones to its blossoms. It's hardy in Oregon so you too can have a "naughty" plant in your garden, if you dare.

Finally, there is the giant Corpse flower, the towering and foul-smelling *Amorphophyallus titanum* (a-mor-fo-FAL-lus ti-TAN-um). The name literally means deformed phallus and refers to the tubers. This is a monster plant. It has large rhizomes that weigh up to 15 pounds each and produces a large maroon spathe up to five feet tall around a prominent white spadix atop a three-foot stem.

164

Seasonal Plants

Conifers

During the December holidays we seem to be more aware of conifers than at other times of the year, and I am reminded again of the problems with common names. If I tell you I put a cedar swag on my front door in December, what would you visualize? Depending upon where you live in the country, you might see a swag made from Virginia or red cedar (*Juniperus virginiana*), western red cedar (*Thuja plicata*), Port Orford cedar (*Chamaecyparis lawsoniana*) or yellow cedar (*Chamaecyparis nootkatensis*). Did you notice there is not a true cedar in the bunch? Here's a perfect example of the confusion common names can cause. Let's look at what are and are not cedars.

One thing these so called cedars have in common is that they all belong to the Cypress family or *Cupressaceae* (koo-press-AY-see-ee). *Juniperus* (jew-NI-per-us) is the old Latin name for the juniper, while *Thuia* (THEW-ya) is the Greek name for a type of juniper (it became *Thuja* when Latinized). Our native western red cedar, *Thuja plicata* (THEW-ya pli-KAY-ta), gets its specific name from the pleated arrangement of its shoots. The Western white cedar or Arbor vitae native to the eastern half of the United States is *Thuja occidentalis* (ox-i-den-TAY-lis). There's also an eastern, read that Asian, Arbor vitae as well, *Thuja orientalis* (o-ree-en-TAY-lis), that's native to China.

Chamaecyparis (kam-e-SIP-a-ris) literally means low-growing cypress, but is commonly taken to mean false cypress. Members of this genus are commonly called both cedars and cypress. Our native Port Orford and Alaskan or yellow cedars, as I mentioned earlier, are *Chamaecyparis lawsoniana* (law-son-ee-AY-na) and *C. nootkatensis* (noot-ka-TEN-sis). One name honors a man and the other denotes its origin, the Nootka Sound in British Columbia. Another American native, *C. thyoides* (thye-OY-deez), also has the common name of white cedar. (That makes two very different trees both called white cedars.) It gets its specific name from its resemblance to the *Thuja*.

The Hinoki cypress is really *Chamaecyparis obtusa* (ob-TOOZ-a), named for its blunted leaves, and the Sarawa cypress is actually *C. pisifera* (pye-SI-fer-a) meaning pea-bearing. It's a reference to this tree's small cones. We have a *C. pisifera* 'Filifera' (fi-LI-fer-a) in our garden protecting St. Fiacre.

The California incense cedar isn't a true cedar either. It's *Calocedrus decurrens* (ka-loh-SEED-rus de-KER-enz), another member of the *Cupressaceae*. *Calocderus* translates to beautiful cedar. *Decurrens* denotes the arrangement of the leaves in which the leaf base forms a wing that merges with the stalk.

Are there any true cedars? Yes, the three or four species (depending on your authority) of the genus *Cedrus,* a member of the *Pinaceae* (pin-AY-see-ee), are true cedars. They are: *Cedrus atlantica* (SEEDrus at-LAN-ti-ca), the Atlas cedar from the Atlas mountains of North Africa, *Cedrus deodara* (de-oh-DA-ra), the deodar or Himalayan cedar, *Cedrus libani* (li-BAN-ee), the cedar of Lebanon, and *Cedrus brevifolia* (bre-vi-FOL-ee-a), which grows only on the island of Cyprus.

These species so resemble each other that they are difficult to identify outside of their native regions. They all have clusters of needles reminiscent of the larch, but are evergreen. They have both male and female cones on the same tree. The male cones are finger-shaped, about two or three inches long and shed clouds of pollen annually. The female cones are barrel shaped and sit erect on the branches. They take two to three years to mature and disintegrate on the tree, leaving a spike where they sat. We are probably most familiar with the blue Atlas cedar, *Cedrus atlantica* 'Glauca.' That marvelous waterfall of cedar over Jane Platt's house is the weeping form of this tree, *C. atlantica* 'Glauca Pendula.'

True cypress trees belong to the genus *Cupressus* (koo-PRESS-sus). We are probably most familiar with the Italian cypress, *Cupressus sempervirens* (sem-per-VYE-rens) so strikingly pictured in the paintings of Van Gogh, and the Monterey cypress, *Cedrus macrocarpa* (mac-roh-KAR-pa), that is native to Monterey County in California. (*Sempervirens* means evergreen and *macrocarpa* means having big seeds or cones.) There are, however, several other species that are native mostly to California and the Southwest. Cypress have small round male and female cones that are quite distinctive from other genera.

You might ask where the all this leaves the bald or swamp cypress that won the Montine Daniel Freeman Horticulture Medal a few years ago. You guessed it. It's not a true cypress either, but *Taxodium distichum* (tax-OH-dee-um DIS-ti-kum), a deciduous relative of the sequoia and redwood. The genus gets its name from its resemblance to the yew genus, *Taxus*. *Distichum* means two-ranked and refers to the arrangement of leaves on either side of the stalk. The pond cypress, formerly *Taxodium ascendens (ah-SEN-denz),* is now considered to be a form of *Taxodium distichum* called *imbricatum* (im-bri-KAY-tum), which means having regular overlapping parts like tiles or scales and refers to the leaves.

Are you as confused as I am and have been for years? Never fear, I think we're in good company. I submit that much of the confusion can be blamed on the inaccurate and overlapping common names. If "cedar" always referred only to the members of the genus *Cedrus* and "cypress" referred only to members of the genus *Cupressus*, life would be simpler. We might be able to learn the individual characteristics that distinguish the genera if we were less confused by the common names. Perhaps by next year we will, with a little work, be able to agree on what goes into a "cedar" swag.

In February, 2002, an article in The Garden, the Journal of the Royal Horticulture Society, noted the discovery of a new conifer genus in Vietnam called Xanthocyparis (zan-thoh-SIP-a-ris) or yellow cypress. In line with this discovery, those botanists reclassified Chamaecyparis nootkatensis as Xanthocyparis nootkatensis. The USDA native plant website (http://plants.usda.org) so far has not recognized the change.

Early Blooming Woody Plants

Although March is the official onset of spring, we Northwesterners are fortunate to have spring-like shrubs blooming nearly all winter. Let's look at some.

Throughout the winter in our clubhouse garden we can enjoy the charming blossoms of *Camellia sasanqua* (ka-MEL-lee-a sa-SANG-kwa), a winter-blooming Japanese shrub. The genus was named for Georg Josef Kamel (1661-1706) who was a Jesuit pharmacist. A Moravian by birth, he botanized in the Philippines and wrote his accounts of plants under his Latinized name, Camellus. *Sasanqua* is the Japanese name for this native of that country. Around town we also frequently see *Camellia japonica* (C. ja-PON-i-ka) blooming during the winter. This common species is native not only to Japan but also to China and Korea and has been highly hybridized throughout the world.

Also in our garden we have two representatives of the *Hamamelidaceae* (ha-ma-may-li-DAY-see-ee) or Witch-hazel family. A large specimen of *Hamamelis x intermedia* 'Jelena' (ha-ma-May-lis x in-ter-MEE-dee-a 'Jah-LAY-na') usually displays its fragrant, coppery, ribbon-like blossoms in January and February in the bed behind St. Fiacre. This cultivar is one of several developed from crossing *H. mollis* (MOL-lis), the Chinese species, with *H. japonica*. The Latin for the species is fairly straightforward. *Mollis* indicates the presence of soft hairs that are found on the new shoots and leaves, and *Japonica* naturally indicates its origin. The Latin for the genus, however, is not so clear. *Hamamelis* is the Greek name for a different plant, perhaps the Medlar, which we now know as *Mespilus germanica* (MES-pi-lus)—a topic for another day.

Other well-known cultivars of this cross include 'Diane' with dark red flowers, 'Arnold Promise' with bright yellow flowers, 'Pallida' with pale yellow flowers, and 'Sunburst' with large pale yellow flowers. In our climate the *Hamamelis* typically begin to bloom in late December or early January.

The other member of the Witch-hazel family in our garden is *Corylopsis pauciflora* (kor-ee-LOP-sis paw-si-FLO-ra), which, despite its name is not really "few-flowered." *Corylopsis* means that it looks like the *Corylus* or hazelnut. *C. pauciflora* is a low-growing shrub that reaches only about five feet with a spread of about eight. In February look for it to be covered with dangling, inch long, butter-yellow racemes of flowers. Elk Rock Garden always provides a spectacular display of this shrub in the early spring.

There are other, larger species of *Corylopsis* in Portland gardens that bloom at about the same time. One is *C. spicata* (spi-KAY-ta), whose yellow flowers are a bit larger than *pauciflora*, come in longer racemes, and have red or purple anthers. Both of these species are native to Japan.

Blooming a bit later are *C. glabrescens* (gla-BRES-enz), meaning it is somewhat covered with tiny hairs, and *C. sinensis* (sye-NEN-sis) from China. *Glabrescens,* a native of Japan and Korea, is the tallest shrub of the genus growing to about 15 feet. Its pale yellow blooms appear in mid- to late-spring. *C. sinensis* is now considered to be synonymous with *C. willmottiae* (will-MOT-eeee) and *C. veitchiana* (veetch-ee-AY-na), which previously were considered separate species.

Willmottiae with its feminine ending is named for Miss Ellen Ann Willmott (1860-1934), a flamboyantly famous English amateur gardener. *Veitchiana* honors the famous English nurserymen, James Veitch and his son John Gould Veitch, who introduced hundreds of plants gathered by the great plant explorers into the trade over a 106-year period ending in 1924. This species produces three-inch long racemes of lemon yellow flowers in mid spring.

A favorite winter bloomer of mine at Elk Rock Garden is *Chimonanthus praecox* (kye-moh-NAN-thus PRE-kox). This tall arching shrub, whose name literally means "winter flower" from the Greek *cheimon* (winter) and *anthos* (flower), is commonly called Wintersweet because its waxy, pale yellow blooms are extremely fragrant. *Praecox* is Latin for "very early" as in winter-flowering. Plant this one near a drive or walkway where you can get near it during the cold days of January and February. It will cheer your soul and make you forget the dreary weather.

Another early-blooming charmer to cheer your late winter blues is *Edgeworthia chrysantha* (ej-WERTH-ee-a kris-AN-tha), the paper bush. As you can tell from the specific name, this uncommon shrub has golden flowers. These cluster in spherical heads that dangle off bare branches like jewels. The generic name honors an amateur botanist who worked for the East India Company named Michael Pakenham Edgeworth. You may find this plant listed as *E. papyrifera* (pa-pir-If-era). The experts can't seem to agree on which name supercedes the other. *Papyrifera*, however, describes the use of this plant as a source of paper fiber. This Chinese shrub has an openly rounded habit and grows eventually to about five feet tall and wide. It is listed as hardy in Zones 8 to 10. Once thought "iffy" in Portland, it has survived up at the Platt garden for a number of years and is doing well at Elk Rock.

Until my *Edgeworthia* blooms (next year, I hope), the early spring winner in my garden is *Rhododendron mucronulatum* (R. moo-kron-yew-LAY-tum). I can count on this hardy deciduous *Rhododendron* to put out masses of bright pink blooms each February, long before the leaves appear. Even heavy snow can't deter this native of E. Russia, Mongolia, and Northern China. *Mucronulatum* indicates the presence of a small point at the tip of the leaf. This is a well-behaved shrub that grows to about five feet in an upright manner. The flowers, borne singly, are generally a pinkish purple or occasionally white. I have the cultivar 'Cornell Pink' which has very bright pink flowers. Another advantage of this *Rhododendron* is that it enjoys full sun unlike so many of its genus.

Well, I could go on and on and talk about viburnums, daphnes, sarcococcas, and more plants that can brighten your Portland winter garden but I think you get the idea. We are most fortunate to live in a climate where shrubs can flower literally twelve months of the year. Don't let the grey skies of winter get you down. Add some of these winter charmers to your garden and enjoy.

The Ephemerals

At the end of summer when the bulb catalogs begin to arrive, our attention is generally drawn to the big, splashy daffodils and tulips, and we order them by the dozens. But in the spring, I find I'm most smitten by the ephemeral bulbs with their smaller more delicate blooms and foliage. What do I mean by ephemeral bulbs? These are the smaller, less showy bulbs like *Fritillaria, Chionodoxa,* and *Erythronium,* to name a few. Let's take a look a some of these little charmers and try to pick up some botanical Latin along the way.

Usually the first to bloom in our area is *Eranthis hyemalis* (e-RAN-this hye-e-MAY-lis), a member of the *Ranunculaceae* that blooms in January. The generic name comes from the Greek *er* (spring) and *anthos* (flower). *Hyemalis* in Latin means "of winter" or winter-flowering. A native of southern France and Bulgaria, this little yellow-flowered relative of the buttercup grows from tubers and is hardy from Zones 4 to 9.

Although *E. hyemalis* is the species most often offered for sale, there is another yellow-flowered species with slightly larger flowers, *E. cilicica* (see-LEE-see-a) from Cilicia an ancient region of southern Asia Minor. A hybrid of these two species called *E. x tubergenii* 'Guinea Gold' (too-ber-JEN-ee-eye) has golden flowers and bronze-green leaves. It was named for the Dutch bulb nursery van Tubergen. *E. pinnatifida* (pin-nat-TIFF-i-da) is a white-flowered species from Japan. The name, of course, describes its leaves that are divided like a feather.

Chionodoxa (kye-oh-noh-DOX-a) is a charming early spring bulb from the Lily family that's often overlooked. Its name comes from the Greek *chion* (snow) and *doxa* (glory) hence the common name Glory of the snow. *C. forbesii* (FORBS-ee-eye), which is often sold as *C. luciliae,* is from Turkey and is hardy from Zones 3 to 7. Growing only to about 11 inches, it bears several blue star-shaped flowers with white centers in racemes. Pink and white-flowering hybrids have also been developed. The true species *C. luciliae* (loo-SIL-ee-eye), named for Lucile Boissier the wife of its discoverer, Pierre Edward Boissier, is much like *C. forbesii* only the flowers are fewer and larger.

A small, spring-blooming member of the Amaryllis family is *Ipheion* (i-FAY-on). This little bulb has been variously classified as a *Brodiaea (bro-dee-EE-a)*, a *Triteleia* (tri-te-LAY-a) and a *Tristagma* (tri-STAG-ma). Since the *A to Z Encyclopedia of Garden Plants* still lists it as *Ipheion*; however, we'll leave it there. A native of Argentina and Uruguay, *I. uniflorum* (uni-FLOR-um) is the bulb most often available. Its strappy, blue-green leaves grow to about 10 inches and set off the single star-shaped flowers that are a pale blue with darker midribs. A popular hybrid is called 'Wisley Blue.' Other hybrids include: 'Album,' with white flowers and 'Froyle Mill' which has dusky violet flowers. The flowers are larger than those of *Chionodoxa*.

The name *Scilla* (SIL-la) raises an alarm for some gardeners because those thuggish bluebells were once classified as *S. non-scripta*. They are now called *Hyacinthoides non-scripta*. There are some very cute and interesting smaller members of this Lily family genus that may not be so vigorous. *S. bifolia* (bye-FOL-ee-a) produces two-leaved plants to about eight inches. The little blue flowers are carried on racemes. It's hardy in Zones 3-8. *S. siberica* (sye-BIHR-i-ka) or spring squill is a native of Russia and northern Iran. It has broad, linear basal leaves and produces pendent, bright blue flowers in loose racemes and is hardy in Zones 5-8.

A very different looking member of the genus is *S. peruviana* (pe-roo-vee-AY-na), the Peruvian jacinth or Cuban lily. A native of Portugal, Spain and North Africa, the name notwithstanding, it produces a conical raceme of 50-100 star-shaped, deep blue or white flowers in early summer above a basal clump of virtually evergreen leaves. Hardy in Zones 8-9, it might be worth trying in your garden.

If you want to challenge visiting plantophiles, you might plant both *Scilla puschkinioides* (pusch-kin-ee-OY-deez), named for the Russian Count Mussin-Puschkin who collected in the Caucasus, and *Puschkinia scilloides* (push-KI-nee-a sil-LOY-deez). Needless to say, they bear a strong resemblance to each other. They are very closely related and quite similar in appearance. *Puschkinia scilloides*, or striped squill, has two linear, basal leaves about six inches tall. It bears open, bluish-white, bell-shaped flowers with dark blue stripes. A native of the Caucasus,

176

Turkey, and northern Iran and Iraq, it's hardy in Zones 3-9. The flowers are about a half inch across. *Scilla puschkinioides* also grows to about six inches, has basal leaves, and bears white to pale blue, starry flowers with dark blue stripes in short racemes. The differences between the two are minor and probably not immediately noticeable.

In my garden *Erythronium dens-canis* (erh-ith-ROH-nee-um dens-KA-nis) begins to bloom in late February or early March. The origin of the generic name is vague, but *dens-canis* means dog-tooth. This is the European dog-tooth violet. Its leaves are marbled with dark red or brown and it bears single pink, white or lilac flowers with purple anthers. A number of cultivars have been developed including: 'Lilac Wonder' with purple flowers each bearing a brown spot at the base of the petal; 'Pink Perfection' with clear pink flowers; 'Purple King' with rich plum flowers with white and brown stripes at the centers; and 'Snowflake' and 'White Splendor' with white flowers.

Oregon has a number of native members of the genus. *E. grandiflorum* (gran-di-FLO-rum), the Glacier lily, with its bright yellow flowers on short stems is one. *E. oregonum* (or-e-GOH-num), that is white to pale pink with yellow inside and reddish brown outside, is another. It has spotted leaves and grows west of the Cascades. Also white with yellow centers are the flowers of *E. montanum* (mon-TAN-um). Its leaves, however, have no spots on them. It grows from Mt. Hood into northern British Columbia.

E. hendersonii (hen-der-SON-ee-eye) and *E. revolutum* (re-voh-LOO-tum) are both pink-flowering. *E. hendersonii* has red-purple petals with dark purple at the base. Their leaves are spotted with fawn and they grow in the oak woods of southern Oregon barely reaching into California. *E. revolutum*, whose name refers to the way the perianth lobes turn back, is known both as the Western trout lily and as the Coast fawn lily. [*The perianth is the collective term for the corolla and calyx when the two are not clearly differentiated. Also called the floral envelope.*] The latter name is probably more descriptive of its habitat in the conifer forests along the coast from British Columbia to northern California. It has rose-red petals with a yellow base and leaves spotted with fawn.

I've had trouble growing *E. grandiflorum* in my garden, but *E. dens-canis, E. revolutum,* and *E. oregonum* do very well in a partially shaded bed that has fairly wet soil all the time. All of these *Erythronium* species are hardy through

177

a wide range from Zones 3 to 9 except *E. revolutum* which has a cold limit of Zone 5.

Fritillaria (fri-ti-LAY-ree-a), another member of the Lily family, is another of the ephemeral bulbs frequently offered. Its name comes from the Latin *fritillus* (a dicebox) and alludes to the checkered flowers of several species in the genus. There are nearly 100 species in the genus and not all of them would qualify as ephemeral. *Fritillaria imperalis*, the Crown imperial, grows to about three feet, for example.

F. meleagris (me-lee-AH-gris) or checkered lily is one that's readily available from catalogs and is fairly easy to grow. A European native hardy in Zones 3-8, it can be easily naturalized in the grass or grown in your rock garden. It produces blue-gray grass-like leaves followed by purple to white, nodding, bell-shaped flowers that are strongly checkered with dark pink. They grow about 12 inches tall.

F. lanceolata (lan-see-oh-LAY-ta) now classified by some as *F. affinis* (a-FYE-niss) is native to the coast between California and British Columbia and is found in the Columbia Gorge. *Lanceolata* refers to the lance-shape of the leaves while *affinis* means it is related to other species. It will probably grow in your garden in a partially shaded or woodland garden if you can find it in a native plant nursery where it has been nursery grown. It grows from one to three feet tall and has bowl-shaped, purple-brown flowers, that are mottled with green and purple spots, and is hardy in Zones 7-9.

F. pudica (POO-di-ka), whose name means bashful, is our shyly nodding Yellow bells. It's an early-bloomer that comes about the same time as *Sisyrinchium douglasii* (siss-i-RINK-ee-um doug-LA-see-eye), our Grass widows. [*These have been reclassified by some as* Olsynium douglasii.] *F. pudica* is hardy from the frigid Zone 2 to the warm Zone 9. My suspicion is that it requires excellent drainage and some summer dryness.

Fritillaria michailovsky (mik-hail-OUF-skee) is also somewhat particular about drainage but it is well worth trying. It has pendulous, broadly bell-shaped flowers in umbels of about four flowers. These are brownish-purple, sometimes tinged with green, with very distinctive yellow tips to its tepals, and appear in the late spring or early summer. Again, this native to northeast Turkey is hardy in Zones 5-8 and probably needs to be hot and dry in the summer after blooming.

There are many more delightful *Fritillaria* species and a number of other types of ephemeral bulbs that will have to wait for another time, another column. I would encourage you to take a close look at these charming ephemeral bulbs, as well species tulips and narcissus, when the fall bulb catalogs arrive. You may find as I do that these little gems steal the spring show from their flashier and larger cousins.

Narcissus

Spring can come as early as February in Portland bringing with it the joyous yellow of daffodils. Before we jump into the world of daffodils, jonquils and narcissus, however, let me say "they," "the powers that be," the botanists, don't always agree on the classification of plants. Discrepancies appear when you look at more than one source. During my research for this column, I looked at *Hortus Third*, Griffith's *Index of Garden Plants*, the Phillips and Rix *Random House Book of Bulbs*, and the *AHS A to Z Encyclopedia of Garden Plants*. They all varied slightly on what were species and what were subspecies of other species. Depending on the publication date of your sources, they probably won't always agree on which genera belong in which family. So one must be philosophical. Pick a source or sources you like. Historically I have relied on the family groupings used in *Hortus Third* (they are broader), but I think the Griffith's *Index* is more up to date on the specific names. The *A to Z Encyclopedia* is more recent than either of these and has become the new "preferred source" for me. For our purposes here, however, it doesn't matter if *Narcissus cernuus* (Nar-SIS-us SER-nu-us) is a species by itself or a subspecies of *N. triandrus* (N. tri-AN-drus). We are interested here in what the Latin tells us about that particular daffodil—that it has nodding flowers.

Let's pretend we are looking through a bulb catalog. What can we surmise about the various *Narcissus* species from their Latin names. The first one is *N. aplestris* (N. al-PES-tris), syn. *N. pseudonarcissus* var. *moschatus* (N. soo-doh-nar-SIS-us var. mos-KA-tus). As you may remember from the "What's in a Name" chapter, *alpestris* indicates that a plant comes from the mountains—usually from the lower elevations. The species *pseudonarcissus*, meaning "false narcissus" is commonly called the wild daffodil or trumpet narcissus and typically has only one bloom per stem. *Moschatus* means it has a musky fragrance. Put that all together and you have a bloom, usually solitary, with a large trumpet that grows at the lower elevations of the mountains; and therefore, probably doesn't require a scree-bed situation.

A name like *N. broussonetii* (N. brous-so-NE-tee-eye) can give us little information other than for whom it was named. A more helpful name like *N. bicolor* tells us instantly that the bloom has two colors. *N. bulbocodium* (N. bulboh-KOH-dee-um) describes the bulb as being woolly, from *bulbos* (bulb) and *kodion* (wool). The names of the various subspecies of these hoop petticoat daffodils are visually more descriptive of the blooms. For example, *N. b. citrinus* (si-TRYE-nus) has lemon-yellow blooms; *N. b. conspicuous* (kon-SPIK-yew-us) has large blooms, and *N. b. tenuifolius* (ten-yew-i-FOL-ee-us) has slender leaves.

The name of *N. cantabricus* (kan-TAB-ri-kus), tells us it comes from Cantanbria in southern Spain. A North African subspecies, *N. c. monophyllus* (mono-FIL-lus), has only one leaf. A whole group of cultivars have been selected from the species *N. cyclamineus* (N. sik-la-MI-nee-us) which, naturally, look like cyclamens with the segments of the perianth swept backward.

I used to think of jonquils as being the ones with small-cupped flowers as opposed to the large trumpets of daffodils. The name of *N. jonquilla* (jon-KWIL-la), however, comes from the Spanish *jonquillo* from *juncus* (rush) and is descriptive of the narrow leaves of this plant.

If you were to see a daffodil listed as *N. humilis* (HEW-mi-lis), *pumilis* (POO-mi-lis), *nana* (na-na) or *minor* (MYE-nor) you would know that it was going to be dwarf in stature. *N. rupicola* (N. rew-PI-koh-la) tells us immediately that it grows in the rocks and will not be happy planted in boggy area; while *N. serotinus* (N. se-ROT-in-us) lets us know that it should be a late bloomer which might extend our daffodil season.

Another popular group of daffodil bulbs frequently offered is derived from the species *N. tazetta* (N. ta-ZET-a). If you are up on your Italian you'll know that *tazetta* literally means small cup. These then are the bunch-flowered narcissus with the small cups. *N. triandrus* (N. tri-AN-drus) tell us that it has three stamens. In this case it really means it has three stamens that are larger than the other three. These are the angel's tears narcissus. Finally there is *N. viridiflorus* (N. vi-ri-di-FLO-rus). As the name implies, these have green flowers.

Although I haven't attempted to list all of the narcissus species, you can see how botanical Latin can help you sort out the species of a particular genus.

182

While some specific epithets are not particularly helpful such as those named for people, I like to get a firm grasp on those members of a genus whose Latin names are descriptive. Then I have a frame of reference into which I can insert those with the non-descriptive names. In the end, you have to memorize the names, but common names must be remembered as well. You might as well learn to use the Latin name.

Crocus

By February we Northwest gardeners are typically rain weary and ready for any sign of spring. Crocuses are often the first plants that appear in our gardens. A rainy winter day found me looking wistfully into the genus *Crocus*. Imagine my surprise when I discovered that, among the 80 or so species, there are as many fall bloomers as there are late winter and spring bloomers. Given the right kind of microclimate, we could have crocuses blooming in our gardens from early autumn to early summer. I expect the key to success for some is keeping them very dry in their off season as most of them are native to the dry Mediterranean regions including Greece, Turkey, and the Middle East. There are, however, some that are native to the southern portions of Europe.

A number of species are named for their places of origin and have names like *C. banaticus*, (ba-NA-ti-kus) from Banat, Romania, or *C. ancyrensis* (an-si-REN-sis) from Ankara, Turkey, *C. etruscus* (ee-TRUS-kus) from Tuscany and *C. hadriaticus* (hay-dri-AT-i-kus) from the shores of the Adriatic Sea. We can recognize these as names denoting origin, but they tell us little about the plants themselves except what sort of climate they prefer. Another group of crocuses are named for botanists such as *C. tommasinianus* (to-ma-si-nee-AY-nus), *C. korolkowii, (*ko-rol-KOV-ee-eye), and *C carwrightianus* (kart-right-tee-AY-nus).

The group with the most interest for us as botanical Latin students, however, include those whose names describe the plants themselves. Several species bear names describing the color of their flowers. These include *C. chrysanthus* (kris-AN-thus) and *flavus* (FLAY-vus) both having yellow flowers; *C. candidus* (KAN-di-dus) and *niveus* (NI-vee-us) with white flowers; *C. ochroleucus* (oak-roh-LEW-kus) with yellowish-white flowers; and *C. versicolor* (ver-SI-kol-or) with variously colored flowers. In this group all are late winter or spring bloomers except for *C. ochroleucus* and *C. niveus*. These bloom in the fall in Greece and the Middle East respectively and require very dry summer conditions prior to blooming.

Flower color is not the only feature of the blooms described in names. *Crocus speciosus* (spee-see-OH-sus), a fall bloomer from Turkey to the Caucasus and central Asia, is named for the showiness of its solitary blue-violet blossoms that come before the leaves. The flowers of *C. biflorus* (bye-FLO-rus), a spring bloomer from southern Italy and the Balkans east to Russia, come in pairs, while those of *C. iridiflorus* (i-ri-di-FLO-rus), a synonym for *C. banaticus,* must resemble those of an iris. *C. longiflorus* (lon-ji-FLO-rus) has particularly long pale lilac flowers with bright orange styles in the fall. It grows in southern Italy and Malta. The blooms of *C. nudiflorus* (nu-di-FLO-rus) come before the leaves-when the plant is "nude". It's another autumn flowering crocus from southwestern France and eastern Spain.

The crocus with which we are most familiar is *Crocus vernus* (VER-nus), known commonly as the Dutch crocus. As you can tell from its name, this native of southern Europe from Italy to Russia is a spring-bloomer. Its European origin probably made it the easiest species for the Dutch growers to cultivate and hybridize. So the *Crocus* we know are for the most part hybrids of this species.

Can you picture a Dutch crocus bulb or corm? It has a papery covering. This is called the tunic. By definition, the tunic is "a loose, dry, papery, membranous, fibrous or reticulate skin covering a bulb or corm." (Griffiths, *Index of Garden Plants*, p.lix). The appearance of the tunic varies from species to species. It can be:

- papery as it is on *C. vernus,*
- crossbarred or latticed as it is on *C. cancellatus* (kan-sel-LAY-tus), a variable species native principally to southern Turkey, Lebanon, and southern Israel where it blooms in the autumn;
- netted as it is on *C. reticulatus* (re-tik-yew-LAY-tus), a late winter to early spring blooming species that has lilac or white blooms heavily banded with deep violet found from Italy to Turkey and the Caucasus; or
- smooth as on *C. laevigatus* (lee-vi-GAY-tus), a species with fragrant white or lilac blooms in late fall or early winter from Greece.

Sometimes it seems as if the person naming his newly discovered plant has trouble finding something specific to attribute to the plant, at least something that hasn't been used before. Then you get names like *C. pulchellus* (pul-CHEL-lus) a "pretty" crocus from the Balkans, or *C. medius* (MEE-dee-us) an interme-

186

diate or "middle-sized" crocus from southern France and northern Italy, or *C. minimus* (MI-ni-mus) a "smaller" crocus found in France and Italy. The name of *Crocus serotinus* (se-ROT-i-nus) indicates it is a "late-blooming" one. This species blooms in the fall and was perhaps the first fall-bloomer that its discoverer had seen.

The culinary flavoring saffron comes from *Crocus sativus* (sa-TYE-vus), whose name means "cultivated." The saffron is taken from the conspicuous, deep red styles of this crocus when it blooms in the autumn. To help the saffron collectors, this species opens its purple tepals wide. Interestingly, this species is sterile and can be propagated only by division. Perhaps that explains the high price we pay for this culinary delicacy.

Did you notice that we found both some familiar Latin terms like *chrysanthus, longiflorus, reticulatus,* and *medius* and some new ones like *cancellatus,* and *sativus* in this column? Hopefully, you didn't need any explanation of the terms we have seen several times before and, therefore, had plenty of space in your plant vocabulary for the new terms. Learning botanical Latin is like learning any language. You need a building block approach in which you start with what you know, keep it fresh with repetition and usage, and add new blocks as you feel competent to do so. Don't let yourself be intimidated by what you don't know, just keep plugging along and using what you do know and add to it bit by bit.

Gaultheria

One of my favorite nursery catalogs came the other day. It's one of those with only verbal descriptions, and I was struck again by how often we see the same Latin descriptive names being used. One genus that caught my eye in this particular catalog was *Gaultheria* (Gawl-THE-ree-a). Two members of the genus familiar to those of us living in the Pacific Northwest are *G. shallon* (SHAL-lon), salal, and *G. procumbens* (pro-KUM-benz), or creeping wintergreen. Flower arrangers will know *G. shallon* as lemon-leaf. Eight other species were also listed in the catalog. That whet my appetite so I also pulled out *Hortus Third* and the *RHS Index of Garden Plants* to see what additional species they listed.

Some species bear honorific names such as *G. veitchiana* (veech-ee-AY-na) after the famed nurserymen, James Veitch (1815-1869 and his son John Gould Veitch (1839-1870) of Chelsea, England; or *G. miqueliana* (mi-quel-ee-AY-na) for the Dutch botanist Friedrich Miquel. Others honor additional plantsmen including: Scottish plant collector, George Forrest; Director of the Royal Botanic Gardens at Kew, Sir William Hooker; and English botanist and geographer, Frank Kingdon-Ward.

Other specific names indicate places where the species were found such as *G. itoana* (ee-toh-AY-na) found in China and Taiwan, *G. sinensis* (sie-NEN-sis) from China, and *G. yunnanensis* (yew-nan-EN-sis) from Yunnan in western China. *Gaultheria antipoda* (an-ti-POH-da) tells where it comes from in a back-handed way. Stearn's *Dictionary of Plant Names for Gardeners* said only "of the antipodes," which sent me to a Dictionary where I learned it was a reference to people dwelling at opposite points and often referred to things from Australia or New Zealand. This plant is, in fact, a native of New Zealand.

Several specific names describe the plants themselves. For example, several of the specific names describe the leaves of the plants:

- *G. cuneata* (kew-nee-AY-ta) having somewhat wedge-shape leaves

189

- *G. lanceolata* (lan-see-oh-LAY-ta) having lance-like leaves
- *G. mucronata* (moo-kro-NAY-ta) having leaves tipped by a small spine
- *G. eriophylla* (eri-oh-FIL-la) having woolly leaves
- *G. oppositifolia* (op-pos-it-i-FOL-ee-a) having opposite rather than alternate leaves
- *G. ovatifolia* (o-vat-i-FOL-ee-a) having oval leaves
- *G. trichophylla* (tri-koh-FIL-la) having bristly leaves

    Two more species have leaves like another plant:

- *G. phillyreifolia* (fil-li-ree-i-FOL-ee-a) having leaves like a *Phillyrea* (fil-LE-ree-a), a member of the Olive family
- *G. thymifolia* (tye-mi-FOL-ee-a) having leaves like the herb

    Three species have names descriptive of their flowers:

- *G. hirtiflora* (hir-ti-FLO-ra) having hairy flowers
- *G. codonantha* (koh-don-AN-tha) having bell-shaped flowers
- *G. macrostigma* (ma-kro-STIG-ma) whose flowers have a large stigma

    Other names describe the growth habit or size of the plants, such as:

- *G. depressa* (dee-PRES-a) meaning flattened or pressed down
- *G. humifusa* (hew-mi-FEW-sa) having a sprawling habit
- *G. procumbens* (pro-KUM-benz) having a prostrate habit
- *G. pumila* (POOH-mi-la) meaning dwarf
- *G. parvula* (PAR-vew-la) meaning somewhat small

Sometimes the names tell us something in general about the plant. *G. fragrantissima* (fra-gran-TISS-si-ma) tells us it has sweet-smelling flowers, while *G. rupestris* (rew-PES-tris), you might remember, indicates a rock-loving plant. *G. tetramera* (te-tra-MER-a) tells us it has parts that come in fours, in this case the flower parts. *G. hispida* (HIS-pi-da) and *G. hispidula* (his-PI-dew-la) both refer to the bristly or somewhat bristly stems of these species.

Names also describe things that look like something else. *G. myrsinoides* (mir-sin-OY-deez) resembles a myrtle, while *G. nummularioides* (new-mew-lar-ee-OY-deez) describes little round leaves that look like coins, and *G. pyroloides* (pye-roh-LOY-deez) says the plant looks like a *Pyrola* (PIR-oh-la), which in turn has little pear-shaped leaves.

I trust you were pleased and encouraged to see so many botanical terms that we have discussed in earlier chapters. Watch for the prefixes and suffixes that are used over and over again in botanical names such as: *-phylla* and *-folia* pertaining to the leaves; *-oides* meaning it is like something else, or *-optus* that it looks like something else; *eri-* meaning woolly, and *tricho-* meaning hairy. With repetition they become familiar old friends that can take the fear out of botanical names.

Ilex

What plant do you visualize when you think about the holidays coming up? Unless you live in the southern hemisphere or perhaps in the tropics, I suspect holly is one of the first plants that springs to mind. The quintessential holiday holly in our area is *Ilex aquifolium* (I-lex a-qui-FOL-ee-um), the English holly. *Ilex* comes from the old Latin name for the Holm oak (*Quercus ilex)* that has similarly pointed or spiny evergreen leaves, while *aquifolium* was the classical name for holly. It too refers to the pointed leaves.

Although we are probably most familiar with *Ilex aquifolium,* there are about 400 species of *Ilex.* The genus includes both deciduous and evergreen species of trees, shrubs and climbers native to temperate regions, the subtropics and even the tropics. In the Pacific Northwest *Ilex aquifolium* is an introduced plant that has become an invasive alien. There are, however, several hollies native to the east coast of the U.S. and in the south.

Ilex opaca (oh-PAY-ka) is the American holly tree of the central and eastern states. The specific epithet literally means pale or cloudy and probably refers to the somewhat cloudy appearance to its leaves. They just do not have that clear brilliant green color of the English holly. *I. opaca* does bear traditional red berries. *(Zones 5-9)*

Another U.S. native is *I. glabra* (GLA-bra). This shrubby Inkberry, that grows to about 6 feet, has smooth (as its name implies), shiny, evergreen, unpointed leaves that are about half the size of our holly. Its berries are small and black. *(Zones 5-9)*

Ilex cassine (KAS-si-ne) commonly called the Dahoon holly is another evergreen native. The name is actually the Native American one for this rounded tree from the southeastern region. It too has small, oblong evergreen leaves with no points and red to orange-yellow berries. Growing to about 30 feet, it is adaptable to wet conditions. *(Zones 8-9)*

Also native to the southeastern region from Virginia to Texas is *Ilex vomitoria* (vo-mi-TOR-ee-a). It gets its unfortunate name from the reaction people have to eating its berries. Better known in the South as Yaupon holly, it is used extensively as a screening shrub much like our Cherry laurel. It is evergreen, grows to 15 or 20 feet, has shallowly toothed oval leaves and persistent red fruit. *(Zones 8-10)*

There are a couple of deciduous hollies native to the central and eastern portions of the country. One is *I. decidua* (dee-SID-yew-a). Known as Possumhaw, its leaves are neither thick nor shiny like the evergreen species. This holly, and particularly a selection called 'Warren Red,' is grown for its persistent red berries that hang on long after the leaves fall. *(Zones 5-9)*

I. verticillata (ver-tiss-sil-LAY-ta) or Winterberry is another deciduous American holly. Its name means its leaves are whorled about the stems. It forms a large suckering shrub or small tree that is grown for the red berries that last well into the winter months. (Zones 5-8) As you probably know, hollies are dioecious (having male and female flowers on separate plants). In order to get berries, you need a male plant nearby to fertilize the female flowers. Be sure to purchase a male pollinator when you buy any holly. Small, somewhat inconspicuous male pollinators are readily available. 'Winter Red' is one of the best female selections of this species. Another, sold both as *I verticillata* 'Nana' and 'Red Sprite,' is a nice small rounded female shrub.

Ilex 'Sparkleberry' is one of the best loved of the deciduous hollies. It is the result of a cross between *I. verticillata* and the Japanese winterberry, *I. serrata* (ser-RAY-ta). *I. serrata,* native to the Sichuhan region of China and Japan, gets its name from its saw-toothed leaves. It forms a shrubby bush up to about 15 feet. Although it typically bears bright red fruits, it can sometimes have yellow berries. *(Zones 5-7)*

There are some evergreen hollies from Asia that are nice additions to our gardens. I like *I. crenata* (kre-NAY-ta) and its cultivars as substitutes for boxwood *(Buxus sp.)* The species, which is native to Japan and Korea, has small, shiny, ovate, evergreen leaves which are minutely scalloped (hence its name) and very reminiscent of boxwood in appearance. It can grow to about 15 feet, but is easily pruned if a smaller bush or hedge is desired. *I. crenata* 'Convexa' is a lovely female shrub with small, dark green leaves which roll under slightly giving

194

the leaf a convex form. It makes a very nice backdrop in the garden. I use it a lot in winter floral arrangements as filler.

There are a number of dwarf cultivars of this species which add an architectural element to a garden. 'Dwarf Pagoda' is probably one of the best known. Ten years ago I planted a number of these in my garden. At the time they were about five inches tall. Today they range from three to five feet tall and are very vertical. As dark green pillars they add definition and visual impact to a narrow garden along the back of the house.

The Chinese holly, *Ilex cornuta* (kor-NEW-ta), meaning horned, is another nice ornamental holly. The species is named for the long spines (or horns) on its evergreen leaves that can be fairly vicious. The leaves of the cultivar 'Burfordii,' however, have only one terminal spine making it much nicer to be around. This holly also produces lovely large red to red-orange berries. If this selection's 12 to 15 foot height is too tall for your garden, there is 'Dwarf Burford' that grows slowly to about eight feet. *(Zones 7-9)*

I chose these hollies to discuss because they all fit the idea of holly as holiday decorations. Now just for fun, let's look at some other *Ilex* species just to practice our botanical Latin skills. For example, there are some species that are described by their colors: *I. cinerea* (si-NEE-ree-a) gray, *I. corallina* (kor-al-LIE-na) coral-red, *I. purpurea* (pur-PUR-ee-a) purple, and *I. luecoclada* (lew-koh-KLA-da) having white branches.

Others are described by a resemblance to another plant: *I. myrtifolia* (myr-ti-FOL-ee-a) has leaves like a myrtle, and *I. nothofagifolia* (noh-thoh-fay-ji-FOL-ee-a) has leaves like the southern beech, *Nothofagus*. *I. latifolia* (la-ti-FOL-ee-a) has wide leaves, while *I. dimorphophylla* (die-mor-foh-FIL-a) has two kinds of leaves from the Greek *morpho* meaning form.

Remember when we studied terms that mean "hairy" or "smooth?" There are *I. ciliospinosa* (si-lee-oh-spi-NOZ-a) having hairy spines, *I. pubescens* (pew-BESS-enz) downy and *I. laevigata* (lee-vee-GAY-ta) the smooth winterberry.

In past columns we've discussed Latin and Greek root words including the Latin *pes* and Greek *podos* meaning foot and *carpa* and *cocca* meaning seeds. So you should have no trouble deciphering *I. longipes (LON-ji-eez)* or *I. macropoda* (ma-KROP-po-da) as meaning the species has a long or a stout stalk. Likewise *I. macrocarpa* (ma-kroh-KAR-pa) would be large-seeded and *I. micrococca* (mye-kroh-KOK-ka) would be small-seeded.

So, why do we pronounce *macropoda* and *macrocarpa* differently? According to the rules, the accent is on the second to last syllable when the next to last syllable is short. (The "o" in *podus* is apparently considered to be short although you could have fooled me.) The accent is on the next to last syllable when two consonants separate the last two vowels as in *microcarpa*.

The flowers of most hollies are bunched together on very short stems at the leaf axles. It is one of the identifying marks of hollies. But there is one holly that doesn't follow the norm. The flowers of *I. pedunculosa* (pe-dunk-yew-LOH-sa) are arranged on long flower stalks or peduncles.

I wonder if you'll look at holly differently this year as you go about decking your halls for the holidays. Even if you don't, I hope you had some fun looking at different kinds of holly.

Hostas

March has become "Hosta Month" in my garden. It's both the time the Hostas begin to rocket their way out of winter dormancy and the time I frantically look for Hosta-deprived gardeners to help me thin the ever-expanding ranks. Is there a perennial that does any better in our Northwest gardens than Hostas? I can't think of one. Hostas can grow from cute little buns in gallon pots to rosettes three feet in diameter in a year or two. They always come up in a nice round mound; are easy to divide and transplant; and are a delight in the garden from spring until fall. There are literally hundreds of Hosta cultivars to chose from these days, and some of them are pretty "spendy." But it's not the razzle-dazzle cultivars we are interested in this month. Instead, we'll look at some *Hosta* species and see what we can add to our botanical Latin lexicons.

It's the dense flower heads that give the Korean native, *Hosta capitata* (HOS-ta ka-pi-TAY-ta), its name. Although the plant is petite with leaves growing to only about five inches, it puts up dense rounded flower heads on leafy scapes, as the plant's flower stalks are called. *H. clausa* (KLAWS-a) is also named for its flower heads. *Clausa* means closed or shut and aptly describes the non-opening flower buds on this plant. This is one of the few stoloniferous species of *Hosta,* meaning it spreads by runners (stolons) rather than forming an expanding clump. Another stoloniferous species is *Hosta decorata* (de-kor-AY-ta). A low-grower, it has deep violet flowers in mid summer.

Hosta crassifolia (kra-si-FOH-lee-a) has thick leaves while *Hosta crispula* (KRISP-yew-la) has leaves with wavy margins. *H. crispula* bears lavender to white flowers on 36" scapes in early summer.

Several species have lance-shaped leaves. One of these is *H. gracillima* (gra-SIL-li-ma), a Japanese native whose name literally means the most graceful. Over a long period of time it bears lavender-blue flowers on purple-striped scapes.

Hosta lancifolia (lan-si-FOH-lee-a) is obviously named for the lance-like shape of its leaves. This species has deep purple flowers on red-dotted scapes in late summer.

H. longissima (lon-JIS-si-ma) has long narrow, lance-shaped leaves. Growing to only 10 inches, it has purple-striped violet flowers in late summer.

H. plantaginea (plan-ta-JIN-ee-a) is named for the resemblance of its leaves to those of Plantain. It has extraordinarily fragrant white flowers in late summer and early fall.

H. rohdeifolia (Roh-dee-i-foh-lee-a) has leaves that look like *Rohdea* (ROH-dee-a), a Lily family member named for German physician Michael Rohde. This 12-inch plant bears its lance-shaped leaves in an erect clump and has purple-striped purple flowers on leafy scapes.

H. tardiflora (tar-di-FLO-ra), so called because of its late bloom time, also has lance-like leaves. The autumn flowers are violet in color.

Hosta tardiva (TAR-di-va) like *H. tardiflora*, gets is name from its late bloom time. It's sometimes confused with *H. lancifolia,* but its leaves are broader and it blooms later. The flowers are bright purple at first and then pale out.

Yet another species with lance-shaped leaves is *H. undulata* (un-dew-LAY-ta), but the shape is less obvious because the leaves are also extremely wavy or undulating. We typically see the cultivars of this species: 'Albomarginata' (al-boh-mar-jin-AY-ta) with white margins, 'Argentea Variegata' (ar-JEN-tee-a va-ree-GAY-ta) with white markings, and 'Mediovariegata' (mee-dee-oh-va-ree-GAY-ta) with variegation down the middle of the leaf. All of these *H. undulata* cultivars have pale violet flowers in early summer.

Two species are noted for the whiteness of the undersides of their leaves. One is aptly named *H. hypoleuca* (hye-poh-LEW-ka) meaning white beneath. *H. hypoleuca* has glaucous leaves that look as if they were covered with a bluish-white powder and are very white on the underside. A native of Japan, it flowers in late summer. The other, *H. pycnophylla* (pick-noh-FIL-la), also has leaves with white undersides, but it's named for the denseness of its leaves from the Greek *pyknos* (dense). Its leaves are very wavy and glaucous. The deep purple flowers are borne on purple-dotted scapes.

Hosta nigrescens (nye-GRES-senz), meaning sort of black, has dark, gray-green, glaucous leaves that are heart-shaped and somewhat wrinkled. Its white flowers come late in summer, while *Hosta rectifolia* (rek-ti-FOH-lee-a) forms a sturdy clump of erect foliage from which it gets its name. Its purple flowers are borne on leafy scapes in late summer and it is a native of Russia and Japan

A native of Japan, *Hosta rupifraga* (roo-PI-fra-ga) is named for its cliff-dwelling habitat. The name literally means rock breaker. It has broadly ovate leaves and light mauve flowers in dense racemes in early autumn.

Hosta ventricosa (ven-tri-KOH-sa) is a large plant with broadly ovate to heart-shaped, dark green leaves. In late summer it bears bell-shaped, deep purple flowers on leafy scapes. *Ventricosa* means swollen on one side. In this case it is the shape of the corolla which gives this species its name.

Moving from the very large to the very small, we come to one of my favorites, *Hosta venusta* (ven-NUSS-ta). A tiny plant only about an inch and a half tall, it has heart-shaped leaves and violet flowers in mid summer. True to its name, it is "charming."

One can't discuss Hostas without talking about *Hosta fortunei* (for-TOO-nee-eye) and *H. sieboldiana* (see-bol-dee-AY-na). The former is named for Robert Fortune (1812-80), who collected plants in China. *H. fortunei* is the hosta most people think of when they think of Hostas. It is the *Hosta* of your grandmother's garden. Today it has numerous cultivars.

H. sieboldiana is that wonderful blue-green Hosta with the huge, round, deeply puckered and cupped leaves we all drool over. It was named for Philipp Franz van Siebold (1796-1866), a German doctor who worked for a time in Japan and introduced many Japanese plants into the gardens of Europe.

There is another *Hosta* named for Siebold that is much less spectacular than *H. sieboldiana*. *H. sieboldii* (see-BOL-dee-eye) has lance-shaped leaves that are a matte olive-green. In late summer or early fall, it produces deep violet flowers that are purple and white striped inside. The early summer flowers of *H. sieboldiana* are pale lilac-gray , fading to white. If you want the real show-stopper of these two Hostas with similar names, remember to buy the one with an "A" for excellence in its name.

Now that you have studied some *Hosta* species and practiced your Latin, you can go out and enjoy the wonderful *Hosta* cultivars. From 'Great Expectations,' to "Sum and Substance' to 'Elvis Lives,' and 'Abba Dabba Do,' they are fun, colorful, hardy, and, best of all, dependable in our gardens.

Maple Leaves

Ask almost anyone what they like about fall and they'll most likely wax poetic about the changing colors of leaves. I confess I am no exception to the rule. Maple trees symbolize fall's colored leaves for many people, which gives me a segue of sorts into a look at the maple genus, *Acer* (AY-ser).

This is a particularly good genus for specific epithets that describe something about the plants rather than just describing where they came from or who named them. For example, *Acer campestre* (kam-PES-tre) is named for its habit of growing in open fields. This is the maple used in the hedges of Great Britain and Europe. And *Acer capillipes* (ka-PIL-le-peez), commonly called the Snake bark maple, is actually named for its slender flower stalks. The literal meaning is slender-footed.

A favorite harbinger of fall in the Northwest is *Acer circinatum* (ser-sin-NAY-tum) whose name means coiled or rounded. It refers to the rounded nature of the leaves or perhaps to its habit of twining around rocks in its native habitat, the Cascade Mountains and foothills. You know fall is on the way when the mountain slopes begin to turn bright red. The other Northwest native is the Big-leaf maple, *A. marcophyllum* (mak-roh FIL-um*)*. With leaves that can reach 12" across, we can all agree that it is well named.

Several maples have names that tell us they look like something else. *A. carpinifolium* (kar-pie-ni-FOL-ee-um) has leaves shaped like the hornbeam, *Carpinus* (kar-PIE-nus). They are ovate, tapered, sharply toothed and prominently veined. *A. cissifolium* (sis-si-FOL-ee-um) gets its name from the Greek *kissos* for ivy. It has ivy-shaped leaves and is native to Japan.

Yet another, *A. crataegifolium* (kra-tee-ji-FOL-ee-um) has leaves like a *Crataegus* (kra-TEE-jus) or hawthorn. Then there is *A. japonicum* 'Aconitifolium' (a-koh-nie-ti-FOL-ee-um) which has deeply-lobed leaves much like a monkshood, *Aconitum* (a-koh-NIE-tum). This cultivar is also called 'Laciniatum' (la-sin-ee-

AY-tum) and 'Filicifolium' (fi-liss-i-FOL-ee-um). Laciniatus means slashed or torn into narrow divisions (the leaves again) and Filicifolium means its leaves look like those of a fern. Whatever name it is sold under, you will find deeply-slashed or raggedy-lobed leaves.

Acer platanoides (pla-ta-NOY-deez) obviously looks like a *Platanus* (pla-TAY-nus) the Plane tree or Sycamore. Again it is the leaves which are being described. There is also an *Acer pseudoplatanus* (soo-doh-pla-TAY-nus) which also resembles a Syacamore.

The sugar maple is aptly named *A. saccharum* (sak-KAH-rum) the botanic name for sugar cane. It comes from the Greek *sakcharon* meaning the juice of the sugar cane. The sugar maple is, of course, the source of maple syrup. There is also an *A. saccharinum* (sak-a-RYE-num) meaning sugary. This maple is the silver maple of eastern United States and it too has sweet sap.

Acer palmatum (pal-MAY-tum) has leaves shaped like the palm of a hand. The name *A. rufinerve* (roof-i-NER-ve) literally means red veined and describes the red hairs on the leaf veins. Also describing leaf coloration is *A. griseum* (GRISS-ee-um) which means grey. It describes the greyish undersides of the leaves of the Paper-bark maple.

The mountain maple of eastern North America is called *A. spicatum* (spi-KAY-tum) for its flowers that are borne upright in panicles while *A. triflorum* (tri-FLO-rum) bears its flowers in clusters of three. We could look at the many Japanese maple cultivars which also have descriptive names, but I think we'll stop with these species. Take at look at the names when you visit nurseries and see how many you can decipher.

Winter Wonders

The "Snowbirds" will tell you that Portland in the winter is gray, dreary, and damp with no redeeming qualities. Hence they head for the desert and the sun. They are, however, only partially correct. It does get gray and downright wet in a normal year. But it's never truly dreary because there are always things in bloom to cheer one's soul.

As I write this column in early December I can look out my kitchen window and enjoy a lovely white *Camellia sasanqua* (kam-EEl-ee-a sa-SAN-kwa) that has been blooming for a couple of months. The genus was named for Georg Josef Kamel (1661-1706), a Jesuit pharmacist from Moravia who wrote about plants he found in the Philippines. His account was published in 1704 by a friend in England under the Latinized form of his name, *Camellus*. The specific epithet is a Japanese name. We can also see early-blooming Japanese camellias, *C. japonica* (ja-PON-i-ka). It is, of course, the Chinese camellia, *C. sinensis* (si-NEN-sis) that is the source for tea leaves.

Right outside my study window (just over the shoulder of my computer) a *Mahonia x media* 'Arthur Menzies' (ma-HOH-nee-a x MEE-dee-a) has come into bloom. The Annas hummingbirds found its bright yellow spikes even before I realized there were any open blooms. A member of the Barberry family, it was named for Bernard M'Mahon (1775-1816) an American horticulturist. The *"x"* indicates it is a hybrid from a cross of two *Mahonia* species: *japonica* and *lomariifolia* (lo-ma-ree-i-FOL-ee-a). *Media* means intermediate or between the parents. Lomariifolia literally means it has leaves like a *Lomaria* (which is the fern now known as *Blechnum* (BLEK-num), the hard fern. This parent is the taller species, growing from 12 to 40 feet! *M. japonica* grows 6-10 feet. My cultivar 'Arthur Menzies' grows somewhere in between the parents to, hopefully, 12 to 15 feet.

By Christmas time the various *Sarcococca* (sar-koh-KOH-ka) species will be in fragrant bloom. The name comes from the Greek *sarcos* "flesh" and *kokkos* "berry" and describes the fleshy fruits. Sometimes called Christmas box, this evergreen has shiny elliptical leaves and very fragrant white flowers in winter. In my garden it's *S. confusa* that blooms at Christmas. I suppose its name came from being confused with other species like *S. ruscifolia* (rus-si-FOL-ee-a) which it resembles except that it has blue-black fruit instead of red. The leaves of *S. ruscifolia* must have looked like those of *Ruscus* (RUS-kus), a member of the Lily family, to its describer. A lower-growing species is *S. hookeriana* (hoo-ker-ee-AY-na), named for Sir Joseph Dalton Hooker (1817-1911) a well-known botanist and director of the Royal Botanic Garden from 1865-1885).

By January Portland gardens will be aglow with the golden blooms of the various *Hamamelis* (ham-a-MAY-lis) or witch-hazel species. The name is the ancient Greek name for a plant with pear-shaped fruit, perhaps the Medlar. (In some species there are fruits and flowers appearing at the same time.) The bright yellow flowers of the Chinese witch-hazel, *H. mollis* (MOL-lis) are delightfully fragrant. *Mollis*, meaning softly hairy, refers to the new shoots and leaves of the plant. Many of the witch-hazels in our gardens are hybrids created by crossing *H. mollis* with *H. japonica*. These have names like 'Diane,' 'Jelena,' 'Pallida,' 'Sunburst,' and 'Arnold Promise.'

A somewhat delicate shrub in our climate is *Drimys* (DRIM-iss). I have a *Drimys lanceolata* (D. lan-see-oh-LAY-ta), that I grow for its evergreen leaves on dark red shoots, in a container that stays outdoors during the winter but protected from the severest weather on a porch. Rated to a Zone 9-10 plant from Australia and Tasmania, it can be hardy here if planted in the right spot. Mine blooms during the winter producing clusters of small white flowers. *Drimys winteri* (D. WIN-ter-eye), named for Captain William Winter who sailed with Sir Francis Drake, is probably more hardy (Zone 8-10) and more showy than *D. lanceolata*. In its native Chile, Mexico and Argentina, this species grows into a large tree with aromatic bark and produces umbels of fragrant flowers in late spring.

One of my favorite winter-bloomers in *Chimonanthus praecox* (kye-moh-NANTH-us PREE-kox). The name is from the Greek *cheima* "snow" and *anthos* "flower" denoting the winter bloom time. *Praecox* simply means very early and again refers to its winter bloom time. This is an upright deciduous shrub to about

12 feet which bursts into bloom in our area in January and February bearing pale yellow, waxy flowers on bear branches. The flowers are not visual show-stoppers but the very sweet fragrance certainly is.

Starting in late fall and continuing clear into spring the winter-blooming *Viburnum* (vie-BUR-num) species are a sight for summer-starved eyes. Perhaps best known is *V. x bodnantense* 'Dawn' (bod-nan-TENS-a). Growing to about 10 feet and producing clusters of deep pink, fragrant flowers from November to March, this is a winter delight. It is, in fact, the result of a cross between *V. grandiflorum* (gran-di-FLO-rum) and *V. farreri* (fa-RE-ree) made at Bodnant, an estate in Wales. *Grandiflorum* of course describes the flowers as being large while *farreri* honors English botanist, author and plant hunter, Reginald John Farrer (1880-1920).

Another winter-bloomer here in Portland is the winter-blooming cherry, *Prunus subhirtella* 'Autumnalis' (PRU-nus sub-hir-TEL-la). This is the tree all your non-gardening friends ask you about when they see it blooming in midwinter. *Subhirtella* means slightly hairy and probably refers to the new shoots or the flower buds. "Autumnalis" refers to the late fall-early winter bloom time.

In February a bit of botanical sunshine typically appears in the form of *Jasminum nudiflorum* (jazz-MINE-um new-di-FLO-rum). *Jasminum* comes from the Persian name *yasmin* while the specific name denotes naked flowers meaning those blooming on bare branches. When I first saw the bright yellow flowers of this Chinese native, I thought I had found a very early-blooming *Forsythia*.

This year I have an new addition to my winter garden. *Daphne bholua* (DAF-nee boh-LOO-a), which gets its odd name from its native name Bhlou Swa, is a from the Himalayas. Unlike more familiar daphnes, this one is a tall upright shrub to 12 feet. It can be deciduous or evergreen (I expect the severity of the winter dictates) and bears fragrant white flowers flushed with rose in terminal clusters. It's said to be hardy in Zones 8-9, so it should be hardy for us. Mine is still in a container as I have not yet gotten up the courage to risk it in the open garden. Maybe next year.

These are just some of the winter-flowering plants you will find in Portland gardens. I could go on with other shrubs like *Edgeworthia* (ej-WERTH-ee-a) which was featured in a plant profile last winter, *Corylopsis* (kory-LOP-sis) species and other plants including perennials such as *Helleborus* (he-LE-bor-us) species, and *Schizostylis* (ski-ZOSS-ti-lis or ski-zoh-STY-lis depending on your source) but I think you get the picture. There are a lot of winter-blooming plants to dispel the gloom of our rainy months.

Delightful Daphnes

One of the joys of spring in Portland is the sweet scent of *Daphne odora* wafting from a garden as you walk down the street. Unfortunately we are often dissuaded from growing daphnes because they are thought to be difficult to cultivate. But in the wild daphnes come from diverse climates ranging from the hot, sunny Mediterranean region to the bitter cold of the Kamchatka Peninsula in Russia . So they are not a fragile genus.

In general they need a constant level of moisture throughout the year that is neither too wet in winter nor too dry in summer. With our clay soil we must be particularly careful not to plant them in a hole that will fill with water and drown the roots. Planting them a little higher than the surrounding soil level or on a slope will help. Most prefer a shady site that will keep their roots cool and moist through the summer. The deciduous species typically take more sun than the evergreen ones but still like protection from the hottest part of the day. It's also a good idea to pay attention to the mature size of the species and choose accordingly, as daphnes don't like to be transplanted. Virus is the worst enemy of daphnes and is probably the cause of most plant deaths. It's apparent in yellow mottling of the leaves.

I have eleven species and several cultivars of daphne in my garden some of which have been in the ground for ten years or more. Two of the easiest species are the closely related *D. retusa* (re-TEW-sa) and *D. tangutica* (tan-GOO-ti-ka). *Retusa* means notched and refers to the apex of the leaves while *tangutica* is named for the Tangut people of the Gansu region of northern China where the plant is found. Both of these are evergreen and grow to about three feet tall and wide, and both have fragrant blooms in the spring and early summer in terminal clusters of flowers.

D. retusa has flowers that are maroon on the outside and white inside and *D. tangutica* has white flowers flushed with pink. Both of my plants bloom off and on all summer and into the fall, and produce bright red fruit following the flowers. Hardy in zones 7-9.

There are a couple of evergreen species perfect for the rock garden. One is *D. collina* (koh-LYE-na) ,meaning from the hills, and the other is *D. arbuscula* (ar-BUS-kew-la), meaning like a dwarf tree.

D. collina forms a lovely dome about 12 to 18 inches tall with very fragrant pink flowers in the late spring or early summer. A native of southern Italy this plant likes hot summers and good drainage and will take a good bit of sun. Zones 7-8.

D. arbuscula is a semi-prostrate plant with tiny linear leaves. It too has pink flowers in late spring and early summer and also, as a native of the Carpathian Mountains of the Balkans, does best in rock garden conditions. Zones 5-7.

Another nearly prostrate species, one familiar to most gardeners is *D. cneorum* (nee-OR-um) the garland flower or rock daphne. The name is an old Greek name for a shrub resembling an olive. A native of the mountains of southern Europe this species will take more sun than most. It's pink flowers in dense terminal clusters make it a favorite in Northwest gardens. Zones 5-7.

A larger species from the Caucasus mountains is *D. caucasica* (kaw-KAS-i-ka). Mine grew to a full four feet with an equal spread in the 10 or 12 years I had it in my garden. Before it finally died of a virus, it brought many seasons of pleasure as it bloomed nearly non-stop through out the year. The fragrant blooms were white flushed with pink. Zones 6-8.

The Burkwood crosses of these last two species are some of the most garden-worthy plants of the genus. They form upright, semi-evergreen plants in the three- to five-foot range. Some of the best known named cultivars are: 'Somerset' which is vase-shaped with purple flowers, and 'Carol Mackie' which has yellow margins to the leaves. Zones 5-8.

A pair of deciduous daphnes are particular favorites of mine. *D. genkwa* *(JENK-wa)*, whose name is Chinese, comes from the Hubei region of China. It forms a very open, upright shrub with grayish stems. It bears lilac flowers before the light green leaves develop. The species seems to like difficult conditions. Mine is thriving in a tiny niche at the base of the rock garden where it gets very little water in the summer. Zones 6-9.

The other deciduous favorite *D. mezereum* (me-ZE-ree-um). It's name is a Latinization of the Persian name for olive spurge. *D. mezereum* is commonly called the February daphne. A dense upright shrub of about three or four feet, the red-purple flowers are borne along the length of the stems in late winter or early spring before the leaves open. Zones 5-8.

For a number of years I have enjoyed a yellow-flowered daphne, *D. giraldii* (gir-ALD-ee-eye). It was named for Giuseppe Giraldi (1848-1901) an Italian missionary who collected plants in Shanxi Province of China. Sometimes call Chinese spurge laurel, this daphne is hardy in zones 3-9. It does well with morning sun and afternoon shade in my garden. My original plant had been in the garden about three years when I noticed an unusual number of orange berries in late summer. The plant didn't look particularly happy that fall and died over the winter. But it left behind about ten seedlings, some of which have survived many years. Incidentally, the seedlings I carefully potted up for the future died but the seedlings I left in place have thrived.

I also had a delightful nine-year fling with Daphne Bholua (D. Boh-LEW-a), a beautiful winter-blooming species from the eastern Himalayas. My plant grew to about ten feet and bloomed reliably starting in December and continuing into early spring. Although it is hardy in Zones 8-9, two early winter storms two years in a row took their toll and killed it. But it's worth trying again. I'm convinced you can never have too many daphnes.

Appendix

The Basics of Plant Classification and Nomenclature

I. PLANT KINGDOM DIVIDED INTO A SERIES OF SUBORDINATE RANKS:
Division, Subdivision, Class, Order, Family, Genus, (Section - in large genera), Species

DIVISION
Three are of interest to us:
Pteridophyta - ferns
Gymnospermae - cone-bearers or plants with naked seeds
Angiospermae (or Magnoliophyta) - flowering plants

CLASS - subdivisions of divisions:
A. 5 classes within the division *Gymnospermae*:
   1. *Cycadopsida* (cycads - palm-like gymnosperms)
   2. *Gnetopsida* (*Gnetum* - tropical shrubs and *Ephedra* - horse- tail type shrubs)
   3. *Ginkgopsida* (*Ginkgo*)
   4. *Pinopsida* - the pine-like conifers
   5. *Taxopsida* - the yew-like conifers
B. Two classes within the *Angiospermae*:
   1. *Dicotyledonae* (the dicots - plants having two "first leaves" present in the seed)
   2. *Monocotyledonae* (plants having only one "first leaf" present in the seed - like lilies)
Classes can be further broken down into *Subclasses* if the class is large enough to warrant it. When this happens the names end in *-dae*.

ORDER - the rank immediately above Family - names of orders end in *-ales*. Only the scientists are really concerned with this division.

FAMILY - Comprised of genera: The name is formed from the name of the "type genus" and usually ends in - *aceae* [pronounced (ay - see - ee)] meaning "relating to."

Examples include: the *Rosaceae* or rose family, *Ranunuclaceae* or ranunculus family, *Pinaceae* or pine family, etc.

The family is a natural grouping which is defined by a broad range of resemblances - some of which are easier to see than others. Genera are sometimes moved from one family to another depending upon changing definitions. There are "Clumpers" and "Splitters" among the scientists. The Splitters are prone to dividing large families into smaller ones. The Clumpers prefer to keep the larger, more traditional families.

Some families were identified as forming natural families before things were formally classified in our present system. These have historically retained their old family names like: *Compositae* (the composites like daisies), *Cruciferae* (the mustards), *Gramineae* (the grasses), *Leguminosae* (the beans or legumes), *Labiatae* (the mints), *Palmae* (the palms) and *Umbelliferae* (the parsley or carrot family). Scientists have recently given these groups modern names which conform to the rule of using a "type genus" as the basis for the name. The modern equivalents are:

Asteraceae (Compositae), *Brassicaceae* (Cruciferae), *Poaceae* (Gramineae), *Laminaceae* (Labiatae), *Fabaceae* (Leguminosae), *Arecaceae* (Palmae) and *Apiaceae* (Umbelliferae).

SUBFAMILIES AND TRIBES - further divisions of the family are often used in very large families. The orchid family, which has some 800 genera, for example, is usually divided up into three subfamilies.

The names of the subfamilies usually end in *-oideae* (resembling). The members of a subfamily must share some distinctive trait.

If a Subfamily is still considered too unwieldy because of its size, it can be further divided up into Tribes to make study easier.

212

GENUS - the rank that forms the basis of the Botanical Name— it is the first name in binomial nomenclature. (When written it is always in italics and capitalized). The name typically describes the plant, honors the discoverer or a mentor of his, or describes its place of origin.

Members of a genus must share a distinctive suite of characteristics. The genus is made up of one or more species.

Once again, as in the case of the genus *Euphorbia* which has some 2000 species, a genus may be divided into subgenera.

SPECIES - the lowest rank in classification. The second part of a plant's botanical name, it is always italicized and never capitalized. It is abbreviated *sp.*, plural *spp.*

II. HOW TO DECIPHER HORUS THIRD OR THE RHS INDEX OF GARDEN PLANTS

When you need the correct botanical name of a plant, the best sources of information for cultivated plants are *Hortus Third* and the RHS *Index of Garden Plants*, but they can be confusing unless you know the code.

A. You only know the common name, so how can you find the botanical name? Look the common name up in either of the two above books. Suppose you have a Windflower. In the RHS Index you'll find:

Windflower *Anemone; Zephyranthes*

B. Turn to Anemone and you'll find the description of the genus as follows:

Anemone L. Ranunculaceae. WINDFLOWER. c 120 perenn. herb. Roots rhizomatous, tuberous or fibrous. Basal lvs usually lobed, dissected, st. lvs often whorled below infl., sessile or short-petoliate. Fls solitary or in cymes; shallowly dish-shaped; tep. tetaloid; sta. numerous (petaloid staminodes in double forms). N & S temp. regions.

The translation: Anemone = generic name; L. = the abbreviation of the name of the person who named the genus; Ranunculaceae = the family to which it belongs. WINDFLOWER = the common name. In the description of the genus st

= stem; lvs = leaves; infl = inflorescence; fls = flower; tep = tepal (a petal which cannot be distinguished from the sepal); sta = stamen; N & S temp. regions = region of origination. A Z6 indicates hardiness to zone 6.

C. Immediately following the description of the genus you'll find the list of the species within that genus. In the list only the first letter of the genus is used so plants will be listed in our example as:

A. altaica .....(description of the species)

A. apennina....

A. baicalensis...

(Note: *Hortus Third* does not use the capital letter indicating the genus, it merely lists the species using bold type).

D. Within a species you may find varieties or cultivars described. For example: *A. apennina* L. To 15 cm. Rhiz. stout, creeping. Basal lvs divided into 3 seg., each lobed and cut; st. lvs with 3 seg., lobed or divided, petiole distinct. Fls solitary, 2.5-3cm diam., pedicel 2-3cm; tep. 8-23, oblong, blunt, blue rarely flushed pink or white. Early spring. S Eur. 'Petrovac': vigorous, fls multi-petalled, rich blue. 'Purpurea': fls soft purple-rose. var. *albiflora* Strobl. Fls white. Z6.

Here we find two named cultivars ('Petrovac' and 'Purpurea') and one naturally occurring variety (var. *albiflora*) listed. Once again, the Strobl. following the var. *albiflora* indicates the person who named the variety.

E. Synonyms are listed as well. The second name is the currently accepted one and the description will be found there. For example, in the RHS *Index* synonyms are shown with equal signs: *A. hudsoniana* Richardson = *A. multifida* In *Hortus* it is shown as: *hudsoniana: A. multifida*

III. ONCE YOU HAVE FOUND YOUR PLANT AND KNOW THE COR-RECT GENUS AND SPECIES, HOW DO YOU WRITE THE NAME PROP-ERLY?

A. Simple genus and species - both italicized, generic name capitalized: *Anemone apennina*

B. A cultivar - cultivar names are <u>not</u> italicized and are enclosed between single quotes:

Anemone apennina 'Purpurea' or *Anemone apennina* 'Petrovac'

C. A naturally occurring variety: abbreviated var. is not italicized, but the name is:

Anemone apennina var. *albiflora*

D. Sometimes plant names are not as simple as those above because the plants can be the result of hybridization. Suppose two species were cross-pollinated and the resulting seeds germinated. That would create a "hybrid species." For example when *Anemone hortensis* and *A. pavonina* were crossed a "hybrid species" was created. This cross is indicated in the name of the resulting "hybrid species" by the insertion of an "x" between the names. Both names are still italicized and the generic name is still capitalized:

Anemone x *fulgens*

Now suppose you particularly like one of the seedlings and you want to name it and keep reproducing it. You have then made a selection and now have a "cultivated variety" or cultivar which you can name. It must be reproduced by vegetative means like cuttings because seeds can revert back to one of the parents. Now the name would look like this:

Anemone x *fulgens* 'Multipetala'

If the hybridization process continues and you back cross to one parent or another cultivar and the actual heritage becomes muddled, then the cultivar name accompanies just the generic name.

Anemone 'Portland Pride'

E. If two genera are crossed then the "x" is placed before the new generic name.

x *Phylliopsis hillieri* (a cross between *Kalmiopsis leachiana* and *Phyllodoce breweriana*)

Resources

Brickell, C. & Zuk, J. (Eds.) (1996) *The american horticultural society A-Z encyclopedia of garden plants*. New York, DK Publishing, Inc.

Coombes, A.J. (1990) *Dictionary of plant names*. Portland, OR Timber Press.

Darke, R. (2007) *The encyclopedia of grasses for livable landscapes*, Portland, OR, Timber Press.

Dirr, M. A. (1990) *Manual of woody landscape plants: their identification, ornamental characteristics, culture, propagation and uses* (4th Ed.), Champaign, IL, Stipes.

Foster, H. L. (1968) *Rock gardening: A guide to growing alpines and other wildflowers in the american garden*, Boston, Houghton Mifflin Company.

Greenlee, J. (1992) *The encyclopedia of ornamental grasses: How to grow and use over 250 beautiful and versatile plants*. Emmaus, PA, Rodale Press.

Griffiths, M.(1994) *Index of garden plants*, Portland, OR, Timber Press.

Harris, J.G & Harris, M.W. (2009) *Plant identification terminology: An illustrated glossary* (2nd Ed.), Spring Lake, UT, Spring Lake Publishing.

Hay, R. & Synge, P. M..(1973) *The color dictionary of flowers and plants for home and garden*. New York, Crown Publishers, Inc.

Hillier and Sons (199). *The hillier manual of trees and shrubs.* (6th Ed.) Devon, UK, David & Charles. Brunel House Newton Abbot.

Ingwersen, W. (1991) *Manual of alpine plants*. London, Cassell.

Innes. C. (1995) *Alpines: The illustrated dictionary,* Portland, OR, Timber Press.

Jelitto, L. & Schacht, W. (1990) *Hardy herbaceous perennials, Volumes I and II.* Portland, OR, Timber Press.

Lawrence, G.H.M. (1955) I*ntroduction to Plant Taxonomy,* New York, Macmillan.

Lear, E. (1917) *The nonsense books,* London, Little, Brown and Company.

Lindley, J. (1832) *Introduction to botany,* London

Neal, B. (1992) *Gardener's latin, A lexicon by bill neal.* Chapel Hill, NC, Algonquin Books of Chapel Hill.

Peck, M.E. (1961) *A manual of higher plants of oregon*, Portland, OR, Binfords & Mort.

Phillips, R. (1978) *The random house book of trees.* New York, Random House.

Phillips, R. & Rix, M. (199) *The random house book of perennials, Volumes 1 & 2.* New York., Random House.

Phillips, R.& Rix, M. (1989) *The random house book of bulbs,* New York, Random House.

Phillips, R & Rix, M. (1989) *The random house book of shrubs.* New York, Random House.

Phillips, R & Foy, N. (1990) *The random house book of herbs.* New York, Random House.

Staff of the L. H. Bailey Hortorium, Cornell University, (1976) *Hortus Third, a concise dictionary of plants cultivated in the united states and canada.* New York, Macmillian Publishing Co.

Stearn, W.T. (1992) *Stearn's dictionary of plant names for gardeners, a handbook on the origin and meaning of the botanical names of some cultivated plants.* London, Cassell.

Stearn, W. T. (1992) *Botanical latin, history, grammar, syntax,terminology and vocabulary.* (4th Ed.) Devon, England, David & Charles. Brunel House Newton Abbot.

Woods, C. (1992) *Encyclopedia of perennials: A gardener's guide.* New York, Facts on File.

Wyman, D. (1972) *Wyman's gardening encyclopedia.* New York, Macmillan Company.

Made in the USA
Lexington, KY
10 November 2011